W9-ARO-794

THE
BIBLE *in*
AMERICA

What We Believe About the
MOST IMPORTANT BOOK
in Our History

STEVE GREEN

President of **HOBBY LOBBY**

and TODD HILLARD

www.ExplorePassages.com

● dustjacket

©2013 by Steve Green

©2013 DustJacket Press
The Bible in America: What We Believe About the Most Important Book in Our History
Second Edition/ Steve Green and Todd Hillard

ISBN: 978-1-937602-90-1

Dust Jacket Press
PO Box 721243
Oklahoma City, OK 73172

Editor: Linda Cizek
Interior Design and Layout: D.E. West
vector art: vectoropenstock.com

Printed in the United States of America

www.ExplorePassages.com

DEDICATION

To Jackie,

My faithful partner in life and ministry.

Thank you for your incredible support,

for taking such good care of things

on the homefront while I'm away,

and for being the best mother to our

six children that a guy could ask for.

~ Steve

IV

TABLE *of* CONTENTS

ACKNOWLEDGEMENTS

This book would not exist without the generosity of dozens of individuals and organizations who shared their experience, wisdom, and passion. We cannot possibly mention them all, but we must recognize a few:

- Byron Johnson and Britt Beemer

- Lauren McAfee, Amy Southerland, Marsha Bold, and Sarah Freeman

- Tommy Kidd, Jerry Pattengale, David Barton, and Lamar Vest

- Baylor Institute for the Studies of Religion, America's Research Group, the Gallup Organization, the Barna Group, and the American Bible Society

Thank you all for your dedication to this project and the Word.

ABOUT THE AUTHORS

STEVE GREEN

In 1970, Steve Green's father borrowed $600 to buy some wood, glue, and a special saw for cutting 45-degree angles. He set up shop in his garage and paid his sons seven cents for every miniature wooden frame they could stick together. The family business grew and became known as Hobby Lobby.

Steve graduated from high school in 1981 and began working full time as the Store Operations Supervisor. He was promoted to Executive Vice President in 2000 and was named President of Hobby Lobby Stores in December of 2004.

Today, Hobby Lobby is the largest privately owned arts and crafts retailer in the world. The headquarters are located in a six million square-foot manufacturing, distribution, and office complex in Oklahoma City. Hobby Lobby employs approximately 20,000 people and operates 493 stores in 40 states with offices in Hong Kong and Shenzhen, China. Hobby Lobby sales for 2011 totaled more than $2.6 billion.

Affiliated companies include Hemispheres, EthnoGraphic Media, Crafts Etc!, and Mardel, a popular Christian office and educational supply chain found in six states. Steve's father, David, is the Founder and CEO of Hobby Lobby. His mother, Barbara, is a buyer for Hobby Lobby and Hemispheres. His brother, Mart, is the CEO of Mardel Stores. His sister, Darsee Lett, is the Assistant Vice President of Hobby Lobby Art/Creative.

In 2009, Hobby Lobby purchased its first biblical artifact. Today, Steve Green devotes half his time to The Green Collection, the world's newest and largest private collection of rare biblical texts and artifacts. The collection of more than forty-thousand biblical antiquities will eventually become the core of an international, nonsectarian museum of the Bible and will be the subject of ongoing scholarly research through the Green Scholars Initiative.

Steve and his wife, Jackie, have been married for thirty years and reside in Oklahoma City, Oklahoma. They are the proud parents of one son and five daughters. Within the last few years, they have added a daughter-in-law, son-in-law, and three grandchildren. They are very actively involved in their church and in many national and international charities.

TODD HILLARD

Todd Hillard is a writer from San Antonio, Texas, where he lives with his wife and five children. Todd was born and raised in the Black Hills of South Dakota. He received his B.S. in Psychology from the University of Utah and his M.A. in English from Arizona State University. He has nineteen years of pastoral experience and has written more than eighteen books. He is passionate about taking the dreams and stories of others and bringing them to life on the written page.

todd.hillard@gmail.com

One:

The BIBLE *and* AMERICANS

"Simply put, the Bible is the most influential book ever written."—
Time Magazine, *March 22, 2007*

There were long pauses in our conversation that day. In the dimly lit conference room of the Hobby Lobby corporate offices, we watched intently as a series of numbers were projected onto a screen. Throughout the course of the afternoon, we listened, asked questions, and discussed the implications of the data. Quite honestly, the results were not what we expected. Up to that point we had been acting on hunches and impressions. Now we had hard statistics, and we knew there was only one way to respond to the stunning data we had received.

For two years, my extended family and I had been considering a possibility: What would happen if we assembled one of the best collections of biblical manuscripts and artifacts on the planet and then shared it with America? What would happen if we went beyond the borders of our own country to share this amazing collection with other nations? Although we knew that the Bible has had a significant impact on our family, we wondered about America as a whole. Did anyone else really care about this book? If we committed the time and resources to collect, research, preserve, and then display ancient Bible artifacts, would anyone even come? It really came down to one central question: What do Americans *really* believe about the Bible?

To find answers to those questions and more, we looked to Britt Beemer and America's Research Group (ARG)—a premier consumer research and market analysis company that has conducted over 10 million phone interviews over the last 30 years. Britt crafted 100 questions and then went to work surveying a random sample of 1,000 American adults from all 50 states. We knew this sample would certainly provide dependable numbers, since most news agencies only survey 300-500 in their polls. We also thought we knew what the results would illustrate: a nation fractured and divided over personal viewpoints on the Bible. We thought that there would be a sizable group of religious people who believe, honor, and follow the Bible. We also expected that the majority of our country (or at least a big portion of it) would be indifferent or antagonistic toward the Scriptures.

We were wrong.

When Britt explained the findings that day in the conference room, many of us went through a major shift in our thinking. Were the numbers giving us an accurate picture? Statistically, this survey had a margin of error of 3.8% (That means that if the survey found 50.0%, the actual number could be between 46.2% and 53.8%). Since we were looking for general trends, this margin of error was certainly accurate enough. It is hard to argue with the raw data from a professional survey. People tend to rely on personal experience and popular opinion, often shaping their own version of "reality" according to their own hunches or desires. But we couldn't dive into this venture on mere hunches. We needed solid research and concrete numbers.

If you are like me, you might be a little skeptical of surveys and statistics, which are sometimes twisted for personal or political gain. In some cases, entire surveys have been intentionally fabricated to skew public perception about important issues in our society. In fact, some individuals seem to be masters at presenting statistics with a particular spin that reinforces their views whether or not the numbers support them. We wanted to avoid such pitfalls, so we verified our findings wherever possible with similar research done by the Gallup Organization, the Barna Group, the Institute for Studies of Religion and the American Bible Society. While some of the results vary slightly (probably due to different wording in the questions), the vast majority of the statistics fell within our narrow margins of error.

The statistics of our survey were accurate, conclusive and supported by other surveys by a variety of organizations. We were looking at numbers that told the true story about Americans and the Bible. As we studied the numbers on the screen in the conference room that day, several important facts emerged:

1. WE OWN IT

According to our survey, 94% of adult Americans own a Bible. No other book comes *remotely* close to that number. Most homes have multiple copies:

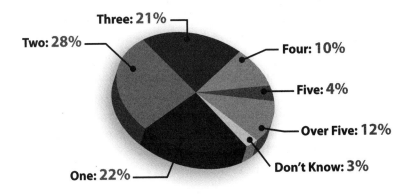

Beyond that, 47% of American households have *at least three* Bibles. We also purchase and give them as gifts regularly. How many Bibles has the average American adult either purchased or had given to them by friends/relatives?

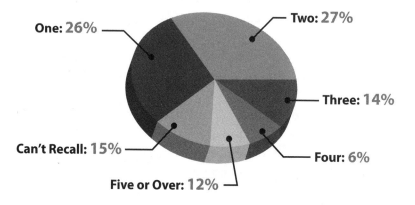

One: 26%
Two: 27%
Three: 14%
Can't Recall: 15%
Four: 6%
Five or Over: 12%

That's more—*much* more —than *any* other publication.

2. WE BELIEVE IT

The ARG survey asked numerous questions from several different angles to measure the level of belief we have in the Bible. What was the result? We have *significant* confidence in what the Bible says. For example, when we asked, "Do you believe the Bible still applies to today's problems or is it something that was practical years ago?" 90% answered that the Bible "still applies." At first we didn't trust what people said they believed! We tried to think of other explanations for such a high number, but the question was very straightforward, and we had to believe that they had given us a straightforward answer.

A review of other studies quickly confirmed the sacred significance of the Bible in our culture. For example, after surveying 1,011 American adults in 2011, Barna and ABS confirmed:

The vast majority of U.S. adults (86%) mention the Bible top-of-mind (i.e., unaided) when asked to name the books they consider sacred literature or holy books. This proportion is more than ten times that of the next most frequently mentioned holy book – the Koran – at 10%. While named by relatively few Americans, other mentions of books considered to be holy include the Book of Mormon (4%) and the Torah (4%). A total of 7% of adults do not regard any book as a sacred text. [1]

Books Considered Sacred or Holy by U.S. Adults:

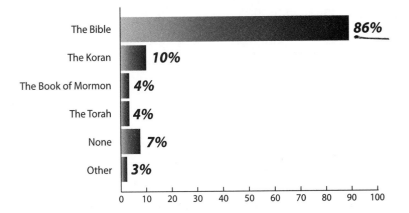

The Barna study confirmed a similar study from 2007, when Gallup and the Institute for Studies of Religion (ISR)[2] asked people to list "holy books" or "sacred literature." 86% listed the Bible, 10% the Koran, 4% the Book of Mormon and 4% the Torah.[3]

We also believe that the Bible is distinct from other religious texts. Only 17% of Americans strongly agree that the Bible, the

1. American Bible Society, The Barna Group, *The State of the Bible 2011* (New York, NY, 2011), 6.
2. The Gallup Organization, *The Values and Beliefs of the American Public, A National Study* (Princeton, NJ: 2007), 18.
3. *"Americans Identify What They Consider 'Holy' Books,"* The Barna Group, accessed November 2011, http://www.barna.org/barna-update/article/12-faithspirituality/31-americans-identify-what-they-consider-qholyq-books.

Koran, and the Book of Mormon are all different expressions of the same spiritual truths. This is a sizable decrease from just three years earlier in 2008, when 21% felt they contained the same spiritual truths.[4]

In order to get more specifics, Gallup asked in 2005, "Which one statement comes closest to your personal beliefs about the Bible?"[5]

- 21% said the Bible means exactly what it says. It should be taken literally, word for word, on all subjects.

- 41% said the Bible is perfectly true, but it should not be taken literally, word for word. We must interpret its meaning.

- 13% thought that the Bible contains some human error.

- 25% felt that the Bible is an ancient book of history and legends.

Barna probed similar questions in 2011, but from a different angle.[6] When presented with a number of possible descriptions of the Bible, the responses were very interesting:

- 24% believe the Bible to be the actual word of God that should be taken literally, word for word.

- 31% say the Bible is the inspired word of God and has no errors, although some verses are meant to be symbolic rather than literal.

- 14% think the Bible is the inspired word of God, but has some factual or historical errors.

- 8% feel it is not inspired by God. It is simply just a book that tells how its writers understood the ways and principles of God.

4. American Bible Society, The Barna Group, *The State of the Bible 2011*, 7.
5. The Gallup Organization, *The Values and Beliefs of the American Public, A National Study*, 6.
6. American Bible Society, The Barna Group, *The State of the Bible 2011*, 25.

- 12% believe that it is just another book of teachings written by men that contains stories and advice.

- 9% don't know.

The same study notes that *fewer* Americans doubt the accuracy and inspiration of the Bible than just five years earlier:

> *A comparison of this data to a measurement taken by the Barna Group in 2007 reveals that slightly fewer adults believe the Bible has factual or historical errors (18% in 2007, 14% in 2011) or that it was not inspired by God (11% in 2007, 8% in 2011).*[7]

To get even more detail, our study with ARG included questions that were quite specific. When we asked, "Do you believe in biblical creation where God created Adam and Eve?" 96% said "Yes." It just didn't seem possible that this was the case! For decades, large numbers of university professors (and the textbooks which they provided to their students) have tried to convince us that humans evolved from apes. After a century of strong evolutionary influence, we never would have expected a number anywhere near that. But again, the question was simple and nearly 1,000 American adults answered with a simple "Yes."

3. WE READ IT... SORT OF

The Bible is a regular aspect of American family life... to a certain degree. When we asked adults with children at home, "How often do you read the Bible to your children?" we found that 40% of parents are reading to their sons and daughters on a weekly basis, and three-fourths of parents manage to do it *monthly*. In addition, if parents are splitting this duty (mom reading one night and dad the next), children may be listening to Bible stories at an even higher rate.

---

7. American Bible Society, The Barna Group, *The State of the Bible 2011*, 26.

On an individual level, the 2010 ARG survey found that 52% of adults read the Bible weekly and three-fourths of us read the Bible at least monthly. This number also includes reading in religious services. Statistics such as these show us that American Bible readers are clearly in the majority. In 2007, Gallup asked how often we read *outside* of religious services. Responses fell into these categories:

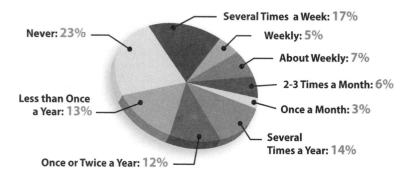

By cumulating these percentages the picture becomes a little clearer:

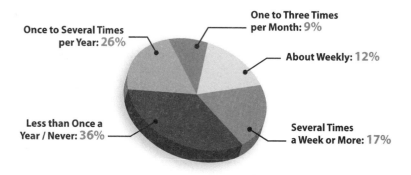

To summarize, 94% of Americans own a Bible; 90% of us believe it still applies today—yet only half of us read it weekly (including church), and only 29% read it weekly outside of church. It appears that many of Americans fall into a sizable category: *We believe the Bible applies to us today but we just don't read it very much on our own.* These numbers caused us to scratch our heads at first, but as we dug deeper into the statistics, a clearer picture began to emerge.

4. WE HUNGER FOR MORE OF IT

We also wanted to know how Americans *feel* about our Bibles. The answers were revealing. When we asked, "Do you think it's time for Americans to go back to reading Bibles?" 88% said "Yes." When we asked, "Is America in more need of the Bible today than ever before?" 91% answered "Yes."

This longing to return to the pages of the Bible is not only personal. We also have a desire to improve our biblical knowledge, so we might share it with others in our family. For example, 84% answered "Yes" when we asked, "Would you like to learn more about the Bible so you could read it with more knowledge to your children?"

The implications are pretty simple: We seem to have a built-in hunger for this book, yet many of us are starving for it—even though it is right there in our homes, waiting to be read.

5. WE WANT TO KNOW MORE ABOUT IT

The survey clearly reveals that we want to know more about what the Bible says. But we also want to know more about the Bible itself. We asked several questions related to this and the answers were consistently high. We have *faith* in the Bible, but we also want to know the *facts* behind the Bible. For example, when we asked, "How much more do you want your children to learn about the Bible and how it came into being?" 61% answered "very much," while 34% answered "some"—a combined total of 95%! Parents want their kids to know what the Bible says, but they also want their family to know the history of the book itself, how we got it, how it was translated, and much more.

The Gallup *Arts and Religion Survey of 1999,* authored by Princeton's Robert Wuthnow, showed similar interests. When people were asked, "How interested are you in learning more about the Bible?" 40% were "very interested" and 34% were "fairly interested" (for a total of 74%). Only 11% were "not at all interested." These numbers were also fairly consistent across different age groups, with the exception that 15% of 18-24-year-olds were "not at all interested" (compared to the 11% average).

Finally, we examined the question that had motivated us to do the study in the first place:

What is your reaction to a 100,000 square-foot Bible Museum where you can see exhibits such as a working Gutenberg press, a 3-D theater with life-size characters, the Jerusalem chamber in Westminster Abbey, a large collection of Dead Sea Scrolls, and see the largest private collection of artifacts and Old Testament Bibles in the world?

Eighty three percent responded favorably. Sixty seven percent of adults are even willing to drive in from a distance and spend the night in a hotel. Britt had done dozens of surveys of this type, but that day in the conference room, he confessed that he had never seen this level of interest in *anything* else!

We were excited, but it was also a very sober moment. This helped confirm our decision to build a collection of biblical artifacts, make them available to scholars in key universities and share them with fellow Americans who wanted to discover the rich background of this cherished book.

COUNTING ON STATISTICS

THE BIBLE IN AMERICA
Featured Expert: Byron Johnson

Byron R. Johnson is the Director of the Institute for Studies of Religion (ISR) and the Program on Prosocial Behavior at Baylor University. Johnson has directed research centers at Vanderbilt University and the University of Pennsylvania. He is recognized as a leading authority on the scientific study of religion, domestic violence, criminal justice, and in the effectiveness of faith-based organizations. His book, More God Less Crime: Why Faith Matters and How It Could Matter More *(2011, Templeton Press), presents conclusive evidence for the positive influence of faith-based approaches in addressing some of the most difficult social problems in America.*

Byron Johnson

It has been said that social scientists use obscure statistical methods to demonstrate what is obvious to any rational person. However, we live in a world where many people hold strong views and opinions, and they are not always rational or objective, especially when it comes to controversial topics like religion. This is why data and rigorous statistics are so important. If you are trying to figure out what is going on in the world and what you should do about it, trustworthy numbers are indispensable. Without data, we are left with little more than our limited personal observations, opinions, and anecdotal accounts. With solid statistics, we can make educated, informed decisions based on data, rather than make guesses based on opinion or gut-level intuition.

On a social level, major policy makers know the value of quality data. I recently completed a series of studies for the Department of Justice on the role of religion in protecting youth from crime and delinquency, while promoting prosocial youth behavior at the same time. In essence, religion simultaneously protects youth from harm while promoting positive behavior. We also have solid empirical evidence that faith-based programs in prisons significantly lessen the probability of a convict returning to a life of crime. Our research has been used in consultation with the Department of Justice, the Department of Defense, the Department of Labor, and the National Institutes of Health. Why? Because policy makers need evidence-based research in order to make good decisions.

Statistics are also important to us as individuals—particularly in the matters that are closest to our hearts: matters of faith. That's why I helped found the Institute for Studies of Religion (www.baylorisr.org). ISR exists to initiate, support, and conduct research on religion, involving scholars and projects spanning the intellectual spectrum: history, psychology, sociology, economics, anthropology, political science, epidemiology, theology, and religious studies. Our research extends to all religions, everywhere throughout history. We are particularly interested in how faith and religion influence social behavior, family life, population health, economic development, and social conflict. We aim for the highest scientific standards, while treating all religion with the respect that personal sacred matters deserve.

Over the last several decades scholars have conducted hundreds of studies that allow us to objectively answer important questions about religion in America. Unfortunately, this impressive body of evidence often goes unnoticed—even by those that occupy the pews of America's houses of worship. As a result, many people have false impressions about the state of faith in America and are making decisions based on hearsay rather than fact. Rodney Stark's book, *What Americans Really Believe* (Baylor University Press, 2008), exposes numerous contemporary myths with solid statistics showing the stability and diversity of religion in America. Other studies continually show high levels of respect and belief in the Bible, as well as a hunger for more of it.

Rarely, however, have scholars directly studied the impact of Bible study on personal and social life. Is increasing biblical knowledge or literacy correlated to real-life benefits? Could higher levels of biblical engagement predict one's religiosity or even one's generosity? We do not yet have answers to these and many other important questions related to the Bible—quality statistical research simply hasn't been done... yet. What we do know, however, is that the Bible is a mainstay of American religion, and it is religion which seems to protect Americans from things like hypertension, depression, suicide and promiscuous sex. It also leads to positive things like well-being, hope, purpose, self-esteem and education. (Please see Appendix A: Religion and Civil Society for a summary of the studies that show these results.)

Yes, data and statistics are important. The more informed we are about what Americans really believe about things like the Bible, and the more we know about how these things affect us as a nation, the more we will be able to make educated decisions about our own lives... even decisions that affect things as personal as our individual faith. You can count on it.

IN THE PAGES AHEAD...

Simple percentages and fractions can tell us a lot about who we are as a nation and what we believe about the Bible. The numbers also reveal contradictions between our beliefs and our actions. In fact, they reveal significant gaps in our understanding. The majority of us respect the Bible, yet we are ill-prepared to defend it when it is under attack. Our respect for the Bible seems to be instinctive rather than factual. We believe it in our hearts, but significant questions linger in our minds. We want to know where this book came from. We want to know about the people who sacrificed their lives for the Bible. We want to know how and why the books within the Bible were chosen, etc. All these things have to do with the history of the Bible. However, the most important questions we have are *personal*. When we asked "What would you like to learn about the Bible?", the responses fell into five main categories:

- How do I read it properly? 23%

- How do I make it more interesting? 23%

- How do I use it today? 20%

- Which is the correct version? 16%

- How do I teach it to my children? 11%

Other surveys have explored the questions we have about the Bible. A summary of those responses reveals more practical and personal concerns:

- Is the Bible trustworthy?
- Is it historically accurate?
- Is the Bible relevant?
- How does it impact me today?
- Why is it hard to understand?

These are questions of the heart—questions that echo our hunger for more of the Bible. As Americans, we are serious about getting answers. Our survey showed that over 75% of us would like the opportunity to talk to a Bible scholar about these pressing issues. Thankfully, many of the best scholars are ready with answers! In the pages ahead, we will tap into the minds of experts to get the best answers to our questions. Along the way, we'll explore what Americans believe about the Bible and history, science, education, and society. Finally, we will investigate emerging trends in Bible engagement, as Americans from coast to coast take new steps to experience the Bible in personal ways. We will also share much more of the cutting-edge statistical research that shows what Americans *really* believe about the Bible.

These statistics are an important part of the story of the Bible in America. But numbers can only tell part of the story. Another part of the story is the rich history of our American ancestors and what they believed about the Bible. Their personal accounts from the past illuminate why the Bible is important to us as individuals and as a nation today. We will even look at rare Bibles from our past; books that lend amazing insights into the history of our country in a very special way.

What do Americans believe about the most important book in our history? We will answer that question with current statistics and research by the experts. We will find that it is loved by many and hated by others, embraced by most of the masses and rejected by others. It is the book that shaped an entire nation… one heart at a time.

Two:

The BIBLE *in* HISTORY

"I have examined all of the Bible as well as my narrow sphere, my straightened brains and my busy life would allow me. And the result is that the Bible is the best book in the world. It contains more of my little philosophy than all the libraries I've seen, and such parts of it I can't reconcile to my little philosophy I postpone for future investigation."— John Adams in a letter to Thomas Jefferson, Christmas Day, 1813[8]

Three square-sailed ships moved slowly through waters of a distant sea. For five weeks, the small vessels had been moving through uncharted waters, rolling with the waves and the winds into the unknown. Many experts had predicted that the voyage would end in disaster, that the distance to travel was too great, and that lack of water and food would spell a horrific end to the fools who pushed beyond the safety of known oceans.

---

8. John Adams, *A Letter to Thomas Jefferson, in William J Federer, Treasury of Presidential Quotations* (St. Louis: America search, 2004), 31; and Norman Cousins, editor, *In God We Trust: the Religious Beliefs and Ideas of the American Founding Fathers* (New York; Harper and Brothers, 1958), 255-56.

But in the captain's cabin of the flagship was a handwritten copy of *The Latin Vulgate*, a well-worn Bible that had guided not only the captain's spiritual life, but his epic voyage as well. Years later he stated his reasons for such a risky endeavor:

> *It was the Lord who put into my mind (I could feel his hand upon me) the fact that it would be possible to sail from here to the Indies. All who heard of my project rejected it with laughter, ridiculing me... There is no question that the inspiration was from the Holy Spirit, because He comforted me with rays of marvelous inspiration from the Holy Scriptures.... I said that I would state my reasons: I hold alone to the sacred and Holy Scriptures, and to the interpretations of prophecy given by certain devout persons...*[9]

The year was 1492 and the captain was Christopher Columbus (1451-1506), a man driven by faith as much as he was driven by fact. History would prove that he was mistaken on many fronts. The world was nearly twice as large as he had calculated. And it wasn't a passage to India that he had found. He had discovered a land mass of huge proportions. Though he didn't know it at the time, the inspiration he had taken from the Bible had resulted in the Bible being taken to the unknown continent for the first time. The Bible had come to the Americas—and the Americas and the world would never be the same.

Columbus's arrival marked the beginning of an irreversible clash of ethnicity and worldviews. The clash continues today as the Bible continues to shape American culture and to influence each of us who live here. The Bible has been woven into our history. It weaves its way through the most important events, personalities, and places that make us who we are. And the Bibles of America— the actual books of our ancestors—represent a unique facet of our history that few are aware of today. Looking at the Bibles of our

9. Paul Johnson, *A History of the American People* (New York: HarperCollins publishers, 1997), 30.

Christopher Columbus

past and reading what our forefathers believed about them gives us valuable perspective as we formulate our own personal beliefs about this book.

THE PRE-AMERICAN HISTORY OF THE BIBLE

When nearly every home in America has a Bible, it's easy to take it for granted. Chances are your parents had a Bible and your grandparents probably had a Bible in their home too. None of these Bibles just "showed up." They are here because of a global process of inspiration, inscription, duplication, translation, and distribution. At nearly every step in the process, men and women made tremendous sacrifices so that we could own and read this book—yet their stories are largely unknown. In our survey, only 48% said they were aware of the sacrifices people have made so we can have a copy of the Bible. Those sacrifices are still being made today as the Bible continues to be translated and distributed. This concept of sacrifice is just one of the elements that make this book unique. [10] Consider these other factors that make the Bible different from any other book:

- It was written over a span of 1,500 years.

- It was written by more than 40 individuals.

- Its writers were fishermen, rabbis, kings, philosophers, soldiers, and even a tax collector,

- Its writers used a variety of literary styles, including historical narrative, personal letters, song lyrics, parables, biographies and autobiographies, poetry and prophecy.

- It was written on three different continents: Africa, Asia, and Europe.

- It was written in three languages: Greek, Hebrew, and Aramaic.

The Bible was also written on a variety of different materials:

Papyrus. Made from the fibrous reeds of the papyrus plant, this durable (but perishable) material has been used for thousands of years.

Skins. Made from carefully prepared animal hides, the writing surface was smooth, could be rolled up, and could even be recycled by scrubbing off old inscriptions. Skins from calves are called "vellum," Skins from other animals such as goats and sheep are called "parchment."

Approximately 40,000 handwritten manuscripts in the ancient languages are known to exist today. We know that many,

---

10. For a much more in-depth analysis of the Bible's uniqueness, see Josh McDowell, *More Evidence that Demands a Verdict.*

many more manuscripts existed. Most have now been lost to time and the elements. The time and money required to make a single copy of just a portion of the Bible was very high. Multiply that by the number that were produced and we have an indicator of how valuable the Bible was to those who lived during those times.

Because of their sheer volume, it is not possible to accurately count all of the manuscripts known today, but we do know that the numbers will grow. Only a very small portion of known archeological sites have been excavated. Private collections hold a stunning amount of valuable artifacts and manuscripts that have yet to be identified. As more manuscripts are being discovered, earlier texts of the Bible are being identified. These new discoveries are closing the gap between the original writings and our earliest copies. Each artifact is one more piece of data that allows us to analyze the authenticity of the Bibles we have in our homes today.

The discovery and study of these ancient texts is accelerating at an unprecedented rate. The dusty closets of synagogues, the shelves of private collections, and the hidden rooms of ancient monasteries are sharing their treasures: biblical texts in the original languages that haven't seen the light of day for hundreds and thousands of years.

THE TRANSLATIONS

Our survey with America's Research Group shows that Americans are both concerned and confused about translations of the Bible. Two central questions are:

- Why are there so many different translations?
- Which version is the correct translation?

Part of the confusion is a simple misunderstanding about languages and the process of translation. About 6,800 different languages are spoken around the world today. Most languages have multiple dialects (or sub languages) and most languages have different levels of formality (ranging from highly technical words and grammar to slang used on the street). To further complicate the situation, languages are constantly changing. The English we speak today is very different from the English which was spoken by our American forefathers. Again, the Bible was originally written in ancient Hebrew, Aramaic, and Greek, so anyone who doesn't read those languages *must* rely upon a translation.

The Bible has been translated into far more languages than any other document. Today, *portions* of the Bible have been translated into the primary languages of about 95% of the world's inhabitants. As of 2010, the *complete* Bible has been translated into 450 languages. Only about 2,000 languages do not have *any* portion of the Scriptures. These 2,000 languages represent the primary language of about 340 million people (or about 5% of the 7.1 billion people alive today).[11]

THE WORLDWIDE STATUS OF BIBLE TRANSLATION (2010)

- More than 6,800: The number of languages spoken in the world today

- More than 2,000: The number of languages without any portion of the Bible

- 340,000,000: The number of people who speak the 2,000 languages without the Bible

- 7,100,000,000: The population of the world.

- 5%: The percentage of people without access to any portion of the Bible in their native language.

Bible translation is a difficult and often dangerous process. Translators face significant linguistic and cultural barriers. In the

---

11. For more detailed statistics and current updates, see www.unitedbiblesocieties.org and www.wycliffe.org.

past, translators faced brutal opposition by those who wished to maintain control of the Bible for political, financial, and religious reasons. It would be impossible in one chapter to chronicle even a fraction of the translation efforts that have taken place across the globe for thousands of years. Still, it is important to note a few of the translation efforts that have affected the Bible in America.

Niccolò Antonio Colantonio, Saint Jerome in his Study. Panel. Napoli, Museo di Capodimonte - 1440-1470

JEROME AND THE LATIN VULGATE

In the year 382, Pope Damasus I commissioned a Balkan monk by the name of Jerome (347-420) to translate the four Gospels of the New Testament (the accounts of Jesus' life by Matthew, Mark, Luke and John) into Latin. Latin was the dominant language being used throughout the Roman Empire, but existing translations were inconsistent and filled with errors. Jerome completed this task using the best Greek texts available. After Damasus' death in 384, Jerome was forced to leave Rome and settled in Bethlehem. From 390 to 405 he translated all 39 books of the Old Testament from the original Hebrew into Latin. It was a major accomplishment and his translation continues to be used today. It is believed that Jerome did much of his work by candlelight in a cave. Legend has it that Jerome was protected by a lion as he did his work.

WYCLIFFE AND THE
FIRST ENGLISH TRANSLATION

John Wycliffe (1338-1384) was born and educated in England. As an Oxford scholar, he was passionate and hardheaded. As a priest, he firmly believed that the Bible was essential for living a life of faith. The vast majority of the English population did not know Latin, however, so Wycliffe and a group of his friends translated the Bible into English from the Latin Vulgate in the early 1380s.

John Wycliffe

Wycliffe's work and his bold teachings infuriated church authorities who wished to keep the Scriptures in Latin and under the control of the church. Translations which were "unauthorized" were forbidden. Anyone who possessed such a translation could face prosecution, imprisonment, and even death by being burned at the stake. But Wycliffe and his companions were undeterred and the movement continued to grow. In 1415, long after his death, Wycliffe was officially labeled a heretic. His books were ordered burned and his followers were condemned. His work so infuriated Church authorities that his bones were dug up, burned, and scattered in a river. Yet today, more copies of Wycliffe's work exist than anything else written in Middle English.

GUTENBERG AND THE PRINTING PRESS

Prior to the 1400s, Bibles had to be copied by hand, a process that was extremely expensive and time consuming. Scribes could spend years making a single complete copy. Only the very rich could afford one. That changed through an invention that altered the course of the Western world and transformed the physical production of the Bible forever. In the 1450s, Johannes Gutenberg (1398-1468) invented a printing press with movable type in Germany. Most historians point to this invention as one of the most significant advancements in the history of the world. For the first time, a page of written information could be mechanically reproduced in minutes, rather than hand-copied over days or weeks. Prior to Gutenberg, it would take a scribe at least a year to make a basic hand-copy of portions of the Bible. He knew very well the impact his invention would have upon the world. He wrote:

> *It is only a press, but a press from which will flow a constant stream... Through it, God will spread His Word. A spring of truth will flow from it. Like a new star it will scatter the darkness of ignorance and cause an unknown light to shine for all.*

Gutenberg would not financially benefit from his work, however. His financier, Johann Fust, foreclosed on Gutenberg and seized all of his assets and equipment. Fust then hired one of Gutenberg's trained assistants and went on to be one of the most successful printers of the era. Gutenberg died forgotten and alone in a debtor's prison.

The Gutenberg Printing Press.

1492: THE VULGATE COMES TO THE AMERICAS

Yes, Columbus discovered the Americas, but it is likely that America saved Columbus's life. He had greatly misjudged the size of the earth and the east-to-west distance to the Indies. It would have been very unlikely that he would've made it all the way if the Americas had not been there. It was a huge voyage into the unknown, but he believed that the Bible was telling him to go:

I said that I would state my reasons: I hold alone to the sacred and Holy Scriptures, and to the interpretations of prophecy given by certain devout persons… I am a most unworthy sinner, but I have cried out to the Lord for grace and mercy, and they have covered me completely. I have found the sweetest consolation since I made it my whole purpose to enjoy His marvelous presence. For the execution of the journey to the Indies, I did not make use of intelligence, mathematics or maps. It is simply the fulfillment of what Isaiah had prophesied… No one should fear to undertake any task in the name of our Saviour, if it is just and if the intention is purely for His holy service. The working out of all things has been assigned to each person by the Lord, but it all happens according to His sovereign will even though he gives advice. He lacks nothing that it is in the power of men to give Him. Oh, what a gracious Lord, who desires

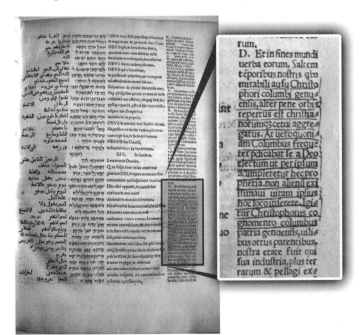

This Bible, dating to around 1516, has a note in the margin referring to Columbus sailing to the ends of the world.

that people should perform for Him those things which
He holds Himself responsible! Day and night, moment
by moment, everyone should express the most devoted
gratitude to Him.[12]

Between Gutenberg and Columbus, the world would never
be the same. During the decades that Columbus continued his
explorations, another development was taking place in Europe
that would greatly influence the history of the Bible in America.

ERASMUS AND THE GREEK
/LATIN NEW TESTAMENT

In 1516, Desiderius Erasmus (1466-1536) produced a
"parallel" New Testament that had Greek on one side of the page
and Latin on the other, but the Latin was not from Jerome's
Vulgate. Erasmus made a new translation using the best Greek
manuscripts he could through assembling six or seven partial
manuscripts. By using the earliest manuscripts available, his
translation corrected the errors that had crept into Jerome's

A portion of Erasmus' parallel translation, showing Greek on the left and Latin on the right.

---

12. Kay Brigham, *Christopher Columbus: His Life and Discovery in the Light of His Prophecies* (Barcelona, Spain: M.C.E
Horeb), 82-85.

translation over the previous 1,000 years. This two-language New Testament was also helpful to Martin Luther (who used the Greek to translate the Bible into German) and to William Tyndale (who translated it into English). Erasmus' work focused attention on the importance of using the original Greek and Hebrew to translate into common languages.

WILLIAM TYNDALE'S ENGLISH NEW TESTAMENT

Early in the 16th century, William Tyndale (1492-1536) was passionate about seeing the Bible accurately translated into the common language of the English people. Tyndale was proficient in at least seven languages. Some have called him the primary "architect" of modern English. He translated an English New Testament from Greek, which made it a more accurate translation than Wycliffe's (which had been translated from the Latin Vulgate, which had been translated from the Greek by Jerome in the 300s). Clearly, Tyndale's work was monumental in improving the English translation. He was well suited for the task, but his efforts would cost him dearly.

William Tyndale

The possession of any portion of the Bible in English had been illegal since the days of Wycliffe. Tyndale's work was viciously opposed by the religious and political institutions of the day. Critics felt that having the Bible available to the public in a language they could understand would lead to corrupted interpretations and weaken the church's power and income. Tyndale had to flee England for the mainland. He did most of his work as a fugitive, hiding in refugee camps throughout Europe. His companions printed and distributed the Bibles in secret, smuggling them into England in flour sacks and cotton bales.

This extremely rare copy of the Tyndale New Testament was likely printed while Tyndale was imprisoned, shortly before his execution.

In the end, Tyndale was betrayed to the authorities by a false friend. Convicted of heresy, he was strangled and burned to death at the stake in 1536. His final prayer was that God would "Open the eyes of the King!" His prayer was answered three years later. When the Pope refused to grant King Henry VIII a divorce, Henry renounced Roman Catholicism and declared himself the head of the Church of England. In 1539, King Henry VIII funded the printing of the "Great Bible" in English.

PILGRIMS, PURITANS AND THE GENEVA BIBLE

King Edward VI took the throne after King Henry VIII. Following his death, Queen Mary began an intense and deadly effort to return England to the Roman Church, earning her the title "Bloody Mary." She burned hundreds of people at the stake, including John "Thomas Matthew" Rogers and Thomas Cranmer, who had, like Tyndale, translated the Bible into common language.

The 1559 Act of Uniformity made it illegal not to attend official Church of England services. Those caught leading alternative services faced fines, imprisonment, and even execution. Thousands fled England for the mainland. While in exile, John Calvin, John Knox and the Church of Geneva translated the first complete English Bible from the original languages. It was a monumental work. It was the first Bible to use Roman letters and the first to have divisions between verses. Many consider it to be the first "study Bible," since it contained extensive notes in the margins. It became known as the Geneva Bible.

Another group fled to the Netherlands in 1607 and 1608. William Bradford kept a journal of the group's plight. He wrote:

> *But after these things they could not long continue in any peaceable condition, but were hunted & persecuted on every side, so as their former afflictions were but as flea-bitings in comparison of these which now came*

upon them. For some were taken & clapt up in prison, others had their houses besett & watcht night and day, & hardly escaped their hands; and ye most were faine to flie & leave their howses & habitations, and the means of their livelehood.

As the religious oppression in Europe and England continued into the 17th century, many began looking westward for freedom. The group in the Netherlands sailed in 1620 and became known as the Pilgrims. Another group, the Puritans, came in large numbers between 1620 and 1640. When they came to the Americas, they brought the Geneva Bible with them.

This famous painting in the Rotunda of the United States Capitol shows the Pilgrims opening the Geneva Bible as they set foot in the New World at Plymouth Rock in 1620

THE KING JAMES BIBLE OF 1611

In 1604, King James I attempted to reconcile the conflict between those who read the Geneva Bible and those who read the Great Bible by creating a new translation of his own. Fifty-four scholars worked on the translation for seven years. They started with the Great Bible of 1602 and consulted the best texts available in the original languages. (Interestingly, approximately 80% of the translation mirrors that of William Tyndale.)

The first copy of the King James Bible was brought to the colonies by John Winthrop in 1630. But throughout the 1600s, as people fled the religious persecution of England by crossing the Atlantic, they brought with them their precious Geneva Bibles rather than the "King's Bible." The Geneva Bible was more popular than the King James Version for several decades. Over time, as more and more King James Bibles were shipped to the Americas during the colonial years, the King James gradually replaced the Geneva Bible in America. It has gone on to be the most printed book in the world, with over a billion copies.

INDIAN BIBLES AND ILLEGAL BIBLES

John Eliot (1604-1690) came to America from England in 1631. Educated at Cambridge, Eliot was instrumental in establishing Harvard in 1633. He went on to pastor a church in Roxbury, Massachusetts, which reached out to the Algonquin Indians, but the Algonquin had no written language of their own. Eliot and his people believed it was their duty to create a written form of Algonquin. Then they translated and printed the Bible in this previously unwritten language. In 1663, the Eliot Bible in Algonquin became the first Bible ever printed in the New World.

Up until the Declaration of Independence, however, it was illegal under British law to print English Bibles in America. They had to be imported from England. In 1709, a man named Experience Mayhew slipped around this legality when he created a parallel translation for "educational purposes" with English on one page and the Massachusetts / Algonquin dialect on the opposing page. It became the first English printing of the Bible on the continent, but it certainly wasn't the last.

Isaiah Thomas was called "The Publisher of the American Revolution." Between 1771 and 1775, he operated his presses from his home, which also served as a secret meeting place for revolutionaries such as Paul Revere and John Hancock. In his book, *History of Printing in America,* Thomas admits that contraband Bibles were printed in America as early as the 1750s on illegal presses smuggled into the country from England.[13]

Meanwhile, Bibles in other languages had been spreading through the New World. Franciscan and Jesuit missionaries had brought in Spanish and French translations. Christopher Saur began production of German Bibles in 1743 and printed the first Bible on American-made paper in 1763. Three years later, he printed the first Bible using type manufactured in America.

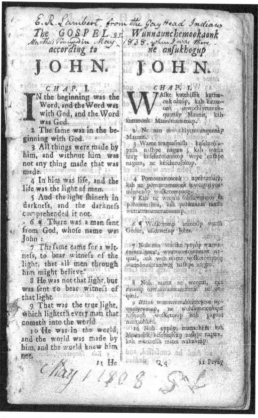

Algonquin Indian Bible.

13. Isaiah Thomas, *The History of Printing in America with a Biography of Printers and an Account of Newspapers* (Worcester, MA, 1810), 365.

ROBERT AITKEN
AND THE NEW UNITED STATES

In 1769, Robert Aitken (1734-1802) emigrated from Scotland to Philadelphia where he quickly earned a reputation among the patriots. Robert Aitken was aggressively devoted to the cause of liberty and narrowly escaped arrest and detention in the British prison ship in New York harbor. When the Congress met in Philadelphia to organize the resistance, they turned to Robert Aitken to print and publish the Journals of Congress for the United States Congress in 1776.

Aitken produced the first legal English language New Testament in 1771. Under British rule, it was illegal to print the Bible in English in the Americas. It had been legally printed in Native American languages, including Cherokee and Shawnee. It had been printed in French, Latin, German, and other languages, but not legally in English. On January 21, 1781, Robert Aitken petitioned Congress to endorse an English printing of *"a neat Edition of the Holy Scriptures for the use of schools... to print and vend Editions of, the Sacred Scriptures, in such manner and form as may best suit the wants and demands of the good people of these State..."*

On September 10, 1782, the United States Congress authorized the printing.

The Congressional Resolution, which was printed in all copies of the Aitken Bible, reads:

WHEREUPON, RESOLVED,

That the United States in congress assembled highly approves the pious and laudable undertaking of Mr. Aitken, as subservient to the interest of religion, as well as an instance of the progress of arts in this country, and being satisfied from the above report of his care and accuracy in the execution of the work, they recommend this edition of the Bible to the inhabitants of the United States, and hereby authorize him to publish this recommendation in the manner he shall think proper.

CHA. THOMASON, Secy.[14]

The Aitken Bible became known as "Bible of the American Revolution." It was greatly valued then, and it is now among the rarest and most valuable Bibles from early America. Though it was not printed in time to be used by the troops, George Washington wrote about the Aitken Bible in a letter which was addressed to Aitken's friend Dr. John Rodgers. It was dated in the year 1783:

DEAR SIR –

I accept with much pleasure your kind Congratulations on the happy Event of Peace, with the Establishment of our Liberties & Independence. Glorious indeed has been our Contest: - glorious, if we consider the prize for which we have contended, and glorious in its issue: - But in the midst of our Joys, I hope we shall not forget that, to Divine Providence is to be ascribed the Glory & the Praise.

Your Proposition respecting Mr. Aitken's (sic) Bible would have been particularly noticed by me, had it been suggested in season. But the late Resolution of Congress for discharging Part of the Army, taking off near two thirds of our Numbers, it is now too late to make the Attempt. It would have pleased me well, if Congress had been pleased to make such an important present to the brave fellows, who have done so much for the Security of their Country's Rights & Establishment.

14. *Journals of the Continental Congress, 1774-1789, vol. 23.* (Washington: Government Printing Office, 1914), 572-574.

I hope it will not be long before you will be able to go quietly to N. York – some Patience however will yet be necessary. But Patience is a noble Virtue, and when rightly exercised, does not fail of its reward.

With much Regard & Esteem

I am
Dear Doctor
Your most obed. Servant

G. WASHINGTON[15]

CHARLES THOMSON
AND THE FIRST ALL-AMERICAN BIBLE

Charles Thomson (1729-1824) came to America in 1739 as a penniless 10-year-old orphan. By the time he was 53, Thomson had served eight years as Secretary of the Continental Congress. He had acquired a reputation for fairness, truth, and integrity. He even created the final design for the Great Seal of the United States in June, 1782. Shortly after, he retired to follow the passions of his heart: studying the Bible and translating it from its original languages.

Thomson was concerned about the attacks of religious skeptics who were questioning the authenticity of the teachings of Christ. So, for more than 20 years, he worked meticulously to create the most accurate translation of the Bible to date. His work was guided by two convictions.

First, Thomson was interested in the "first texts." Although the Old Testament was originally written in Hebrew, he chose to translate from the Greek Septuagint (which dates back to the third century B.C.), because it was older than the Hebrew manuscripts available to him at that time.

15. Robert R. Dearden, Jr. and Douglas S. Watson, *An Original Leaf from the Bible of the Revolution and an Essay Concerning It* (San Francisco, CA: John Howell, 1930), 28.

Second, Thomson was interested in "first meanings." He knew that certain concepts could be lost when word-for-word translations were made between languages, and sometimes word-for-word translations came across as harsh and obscure. He stated his goal in his own words:

> *To give a just and true representation of the sense and*
> *meaning of the Sacred Scriptures; and in doing this, I*
> *have further endeavored to convey into the translation,*
> *as far as I could, the spirit and manner of the authors,*
> *and thereby give it the quality of an original.*[16]

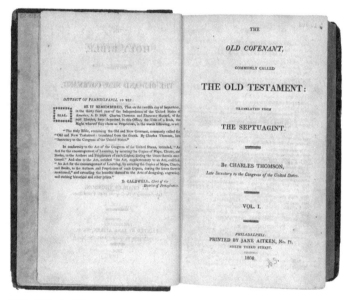

The first All-American Bible.

His principles and the quality of his work set the standard for Bible translation for decades to come. Printed in 1808, the translation was a significant milestone in many ways. Thomson's Bible was the first to be printed in America by a woman, Jane

---

16. Paul Gutjahr, *An American Bible: A History of the Good Book in the United States, 1777-1880* (Stanford, California: Stanford University Press, 1999), 94.

Aitken, the daughter of Robert Aitken. Since it was printed in America on paper made in America by a patriot who translated it into the English of the Americans, the Thomson Bible can rightly be called the first "All-American" Bible.

THE BIBLE SOCIETIES

With the war behind them, Americans now had the freedom to print and distribute Bibles at will. Community groups began to organize to make sure their cities had Bibles available to all. The first to mobilize was the Philadelphia Bible Society in 1808. The New York Bible Society followed in 1809. (It later changed its name to the International Bible Society, now located in Colorado Springs.) The Baltimore Bible Society was founded by James McHenry (1753-1816), a signer of the Constitution and Secretary of War under George Washington and John Adams. McHenry wrote:

> *The holy Scriptures... Can alone secure to society, order and peace, and to our courts of justice and constitutions of government, purity, stability, and usefulness. In vain, without the Bible, we increase penal laws and drop protections around our institutions.*[17]

Soon, state Bible societies were formed as well in Connecticut, Massachusetts, New York, and Maine. The American Bible Society was established in 1816 with Elias Boudinot (1740-1821) as its first president. Elias had been a fellow patriot with George Washington, was a neighbor of Benjamin Franklin, and had mentored Alexander Hamilton. Boudinot served three terms with the Continental Congress and was its president in 1782. He signed the peace treaty with Great Britain to end the Revolution and served as the director of the U.S. Mint. Even with

---

17. Bernard C. Steiner, *One Hundred and Ten Years of Bible Society Work in Maryland, 1810-1920* (Maryland Bible Society, 1921), 14.

all these accomplishments, Boudinot said that his presidency of the American Bible Society was "the greatest honor that could have been conferred on me this side of the grave."[18] The goal was to place a Bible in every home in America. The founders of the American Bible Society were dedicated to making sure the Bible would "abound" (as James McHenry put it). The ABS founders included:

- John Jay; the original Chief Justice of the U.S. Supreme Court and co-author of the Federalist Papers.

- Matthew Clarkson; a Major General during the American Revolution and a leader in American education and politics.

- Smith Thompson; a United States Supreme Court Justice.

- John Langdon; a signer of the U.S. Constitution.

- Bushrod Washington; a United States Supreme Court Justice.

- William Wirt; the Attorney General of the United States.

- Charles Cotesworth Pinckney; a Major General in the American Revolution and a signer of the U.S. Constitution.

The presidents of the American Bible Society read like a list of "Who's Who" among the Founding Fathers.

- John Jay; the first Chief Justice of the U.S. Supreme Court.

- John Quincy Adams; the sixth President of the U.S.

- Francis Scott Key; poet and the author of the National Anthem.

---

18. *Annual report of the American Bible Society, Vol 1.* Appendix. Reprint for the Society by Danile Fanshaw, 1838.

- Rutherford B. Hayes; the 19th President of the U.S.

- Benjamin Harrison; the 23rd President of the U.S.

John Jay (1745-1829) was the second president of the American Bible Society. He was a member of the Continental Congress, had served as Secretary of Foreign Affairs under the Articles of Confederation, and was the U.S. Minister to Spain. John Quincy Adams (1767-1848), the sixth President of the United States, served as the Chairman of the American Bible Society in 1844. He was still serving as a U.S. Congressman at age 76. In a speech that same year, given to the American Bible Society on February 27, he shared his beliefs about the Bible:

> *I deem myself fortunate in having the opportunity, at a stage of a long life drawing rapidly to its close, to bear at this place, the capital of our National Union, in the Hall of representatives of the North American people, in the chair of the presiding officer of the assembly representing the whole people, the personification of the great and mighty nation – to bear my solemn testimonial of reverence and gratitude to that book of books, the Holy Bible.... The Bible carries with it the history of the creation, the fall and redemption of man, and discloses to him, in the infant born at Bethlehem, the Legislator and Saviour of the world.*

John Quincy Adams, President of the United States, Chairman of the American Bible Society.

THE MODERN
AMERICAN TRANSLATIONS

Throughout the centuries, continual effort has been made to make our translations of the Bible as accurate as possible. Those efforts, combined with the discovery and identification of older manuscripts, ensure that the Bibles we have today are trustworthy. Today's translations are not the end-product of the Bible being passed down a long series of sources. Having older, more accurate manuscripts means we are getting closer to the originals all the time. Analysis of the data shows that the variations in the original languages are very minor.

But languages themselves change over time (something you understand if you've ever read Shakespeare). Even though we are dealing with the best copies in the *ancient* languages, it is necessary to update translations, so that the Bible can be read naturally in our *modern* language. This is not necessary because the Bible has changed; it is necessary because our language has changed.

The first modern American translation was done by the great statesman and linguist Noah Webster. He is probably best known for his contributions to education and, in particular, for the famous dictionary which bears his name. Webster knew that the English language had changed in the 200 years since the King James had been translated in 1611. He felt that a more contemporary version was needed of this popular translation, so he worked meticulously to update it. It was printed in 1833. To his disappointment, however, the Noah Webster Bible did not sell well. Perhaps Webster was just ahead of his time, for in 1975 a team of scholars, pastors, and theologians began again updating the King James Version's grammar and vocabulary. The completed work, called the *New King James Version*, was published in 1982, and is now owned by about 17% of Americans.

In the last several decades, efforts to create modern translations have accelerated, particularly as recent advancements in archaeology, linguistics, and manuscript research have made more accurate translation possible. New translations fall into three general categories:

1. Word-for-Word Translations

The New American Standard Bible (NASB) was published in 1971 as a "modern and accurate word-for-word English translation." Translators attempted to be as literal as possible and preserve the word order in the original Greek and Hebrew. Translations such as these are preferred by those doing serious study. Other examples include *The New King James Version, The Amplified Bible*, and *The New American Bible*.

2. Phrase-for-Phrase Translations

In 1973, *The New International Version* (NIV) was published as a "modern and accurate phrase- for- phrase English translation." The sentence structure is natural for modern readers and the vocabulary is less formal. Other examples include *The New Century Version, The Contemporary English Version*, and *The New Living Translation*. They are preferred by those seeking a balance between readability and accuracy.

3. Paraphrase Translations

The Living Bible of 1971 pioneered the concept of idea-by-idea translation, often called a "paraphrase." The translators often take liberty to inject what they think the original writers meant and they use concepts that they think the original writers would have used if they had been writing today. They sometimes use contemporary slang. These Bibles read smoothly and easily and are preferred for casual reading. Another example of a paraphrase is the *The Message*. The top selling Bible in America today is *The New International Version* (NIV), followed by *The King James Version* (KJV), then *The New King James Version* (NKJV), *The New Living Translation* (NLT), and *The English Standard Version* (ESV).

THE LINK TO OUR LEGACY

Modern translations are the most recent links in a chain that connect us to a long history—the history of a nation that is inseparably intertwined with the Bible. The Bible is *in* America—it's a legacy woven into the fabric of our nation with the sweat, blood, and faith of those who have gone before us.

The impact of the Bible on America was highlighted when Congress asked the President to designate 1983 as "The Year of the Bible." On the eve of that year, *Newsweek* said:

> *[The Bible] has exerted an unrivaled influence on American culture, politics and social life. Now historians are discovering that the Bible, perhaps even more than the Constitution, is our founding document: the source of the powerful myth of the United States as a special, sacred nation, a people called by God to establish a model society, a beacon to the world.[19]*

The history of the Bible in America is a strong indicator of what our forefathers believed about it. The statistics tell one side of the story. The other side of the story is told by the books themselves, Bibles that were translated, printed, and distributed through the deep sacrifices of men and women who believed in them. Perhaps the Presidential Proclamation of 1983 summarizes it the best:

> *Of the many influences that have shaped the United States of America into a distinctive nation and people, none may be said to be more fundamental and enduring than the Bible.*
>
> *Deep religious beliefs stemming from the old and new Testaments of the Bible inspired many of the early*

---

19. Kenneth L. Woodward with David Gates, *"How the Bible made America: Since the Puritans and the pioneers, through wars and social conflicts, a sense of Bible mission has united us, divided us, and shaped our national destiny,"* Newsweek, December 27, 1982, 44.

settlers of our country, providing them with the strength, character, convictions and faith necessary to withstand great hardship and danger in this new and rugged land. Their shared beliefs helped forge a new sense of common purpose among the widely dispersed colonies--a sense of community which laid the foundation for the spirit of the nationhood that was to develop in later decades.

Many of our greatest national leaders--among them presidents Washington, Jackson, Lincoln, and Wilson have recognized the influence of the Bible on our country's development. The plainspoken Andrew Jackson referred to the Bible as no less than "the rock on which our Republic rests."

The Congress of the United States, in recognition of the unique contribution of the Bible in shaping the history and character of this nation, and so many of its citizens, has by Senate joint resolution 165 authorized and requested the President to designate the year 1983 as the "Year of the Bible." [20]

Ronald Reagan

---

20. Ronald Reagan, *A Proclamation by the President of the United States of America for the Year of the Bible*, 1983.

Three:

The BIBLE *in* SCIENCE

"I want to understand the thoughts of God."
—Albert Einstein

We are living in unprecedented times. Applied technology is accelerating at such an incredible pace that a raging flood of information and technology now consumes the globe. The Bible and science are saturated in this flood of information. A hundred years ago, the problem was *getting* information. Today, we have too much! Now the challenge is filtering out what's important and trying to discern what is true and what is false.

Science and the Bible are married to each other in several ways: biblical and scientific thought both proliferated during the same time in the same place; they are both dependent on each other and they have influenced each other to an inseparable degree. Also, like any couple trying to find their place in the world, the Bible and science appear to be in conflict with each other on a fairly regular basis. This inseparable relationship between the

Bible and science is one of the most interesting relationships in American history.

The word "science" comes from the Latin word *scientia*, meaning "knowledge." During the classical age, the work of Aristotle and Plato (5ᵗʰ and 4ᵗʰ centuries B.C.) focused on human knowledge. Today we call this area of study "philosophy," which investigates what *we* know and how *we* think as humans. The philosophers of old were brilliant and they did a lot of fantastic thinking, but thinking alone doesn't create facts. Philosophy wrestles with *ideas*, and many of their ideas about the *facts* of the physical world were far from accurate. Plato, for example, considered the world to be "a single living creature," which, of course, the modern scientific community has disproved.

Still, the Middle Ages was a time of progressive technology and invention. At the same time the Bible was spreading across Europe, major technological advances took place.[21]

- In 732, knights in full armor engaged in their first major battle; something that was made possible by the invention of stirrups and the "Norman saddle."

- The horse collar (which placed the force on a horse's shoulders rather than its neck) meant heavier burdens could be moved faster.

- Iron horseshoes came into being, as did waterwheels, mills, camshafts, and mechanical clocks.

- During this time, technologies borrowed from other cultures were widely adopted for use.

- The Chinese had used gunpowder for fireworks, but when the Europeans found out about it, they almost immediately adopted it for cannons early in the 1300s.

---

21. Rodney Stark, *For the Glory of God: How Monotheism Led to Reformations, Science, Witch-Hunts, and the End of Slavery* (Princeton: Princeton University Press, 2003), 143-144.

- The Chinese also had a very crude compass, but medieval Europeans developed a site and a compass card that greatly increased its accuracy and usefulness.

- The Greeks, the Romans, as well as the Muslims had forbidden human dissection, but in the European universities of the Middle Ages, the practice flourished, along with the understanding of human physiology.

All this took place as the Bible was making significant inroads into European culture. Simultaneously, a shift began to take place in the pursuit of knowledge—a shift that began to look *outwardly* for physical truth. For example, Albertus Magnus (1205-1280), and others of the scholastic era, began to look for new facts in the world. They found that the ideas of some of the great philosophers weren't supported by objective observations.

But even with these advancements, the so-called "scientific revolution" had yet to be ignited. What was needed was a method—a way of thinking and a way of researching—that could lead to concrete and measurable results.

THE FATHER OF SCIENCE

Francis Bacon (1561-1626) was born during a pivotal season of world history, and his life altered the course of that history. Though he succeeded as a philosopher, he failed as a politician, and he developed a method of research that earned him the title "Father of the Scientific Method." His contributions are well remembered and can hardly be overstated. The world finally had a template to follow in gaining factual wisdom. Now, when the word "science" is used, it usually refers only to the study of the physical, material universe and everything in it. Frank Wolfs of the University of Rochester says, "The scientific method is the process by which scientists, collectively and over time, endeavor to construct an accurate (that is, reliable, consistent and non-arbitrary) representation of the world." The process is usually described in four steps:

1. Observation and description of an object or an action in the physical world.

2. Formulation of a new, untested "hypothesis" to further describe the object or explain the action.

3. Prediction of what could happen if the hypothesis is true.

4. Experimental testing of the predictions to see if the hypothesis is supported or disproven.

The method was revolutionary back then, even though it seems like common sense to us in the modern world. This simple way of gaining new knowledge led to an explosion of research and discovery. The shockwaves of this explosion in Europe have been impacting the world for more than 400 years.

It was here, at the dawn of the Scientific Age, that we see the beginning of the inseparable relationship between the Bible and science. Bacon was a devoted reader of the Bible and his notes can be found in the margins of many different Bibles. He also wrote his own commentary on the entire Bible. Beginning with the first verse, Genesis 1:1, he wrote:

> *I believe that nothing is without beginning, but God: no nature, no matter, no spirit, but one, only, and the same God. That God, as he is eternally Almighty, only wise, only good, in his nature: so he is eternally father, son, and Spirit, in person...*[22]

---

22. *"Francis Bacon's Bible Thoughts,"* Francis Bacon, accessed July 28, 2012, http://books.google.com/books?id=-8235tQoUuEC&pg=PA391&source=gbs_selected_pages&cad=3#v=onepage&q&f=false.

Sir Francis Bacon, "Father of the Scientific Method"

Bacon was knighted by King James in 1603 and was involved in the translation of the King James Version of the Bible. Some believe that the translation was his idea, that he developed the protocol the translators utilized, and that he followed the translation from stage to stage.[23] When the translation was completed in 1609, King James passed it on to Sir Francis Bacon for final edits. Historian William T. Smedley wrote:

> *It will eventually be proved that the whole structure of the Authorized Bible was Francis Bacon's. He was an ardent student not only of the Bible, but also of early manuscripts. St. Augustine, St. Jerome, and writers of theological works, were studied by him with industry.*[24]

---

23. *"Francis Bacon and the James 1st Bible,"* A. E. Loosley, accessed July 28, 2012, http://www.sirbacon.org/links/bible.html.
24. William Smedley, *The Mystery of Francis Bacon* (London: Robert Banks and Son, 1912), 126.

As if he didn't have enough to do, Francis Bacon also played a leading role in creating the British colonies of Virginia, the Carolinas and Newfoundland in Canada. Newfoundland issued a postage stamp in 1910 describing Bacon as the "Guiding Spirit in Colonization Schemes in 1610." Other scholars believe he was largely responsible for drafting two of the charters for the Virginia Colony in 1609 and 1612.[25] Historian William Hepworth Dixon wrote that Bacon's name could be included in the list of Founders of the United States of America.[26]

Not only was he the founder of the scientific method, but his philosophies encouraged the application of science for the good of humanity—ideas which helped launch the Industrial Revolution of the 1800s. The mixture of scientific knowledge and biblical principles had a profound effect. Nobel Prize winner Robert E. Lucas, Jr., wrote, "For the first time in history, the living standards of the masses of ordinary people have begun to undergo sustained growth ... Nothing remotely like this economic behavior has happened before."[27]

It would be difficult to find any person who integrated the Bible and science so well. Faith and fact were seamlessly woven into Bacon's life from the very beginning until he died.

LAWS AND ORDER

Sir Isaac Newton (1642–1727) was a distinguished English mathematician, physicist, astronomer, chemist, and theologian. He also spent plenty of time in philosophy, but it was in science that his legacy has endured. Newton is considered by many to be the greatest and most influential scientist who ever lived. He was a brilliant pioneer in optics and calculus. His most important work was published in 1687, The *Philosophiae Naturalis Principia*

---

25. *"Francis Bacon's Life, A Brief Historical Sketch,"* Peter Dawkins, accessed July 28, 2012, http://www.fbrt. org.uk/pages/essays/essay-fb-life.html.
26. William Hepworth Dixon, *Personal History of Lord Bacon from Unpublished Papers* (Boston: Ticknor and Fields, 1861) 200.
27. Robert E. Lucas Jr., *Lectures on Economic Growth* (Cambridge: Harvard University Press, 2006), 109–10.

Mathematica (Latin for "Mathematical Principles of Natural Philosophy"). In this groundbreaking work, Newton described his three laws of motion and explained universal gravitation. These principles are the bedrock of modern physics. *Principia* is probably the most important scientific book ever written.

Sir Isaac Newton

Newton was also a devoted student of the Bible. When it came to faith and science, he saw the two as inseparable. In letters written to Richard Bentley between 1692 and 1693, Newton explained how the intricate laws of nature were the fingerprints of an intelligent, omnipotent God:

> *Gravity explains the motions of the planets, but it cannot explain who set the planets in motion. God governs all things and knows all that is or can be done.[28]*

The "evidence of design" that he saw in the world motivated him to search for the "laws" that "govern" the physical world. In the

---

28. J.H. Tiner, *Isaac Newton: Inventor, Scientist and Teacher* (Milford, Michigan: Mott Media, 1975), 233.

second edition of *Philosophiae Naturalis Principia Mathematica,* which *was* published in 1731, he added an important section that revealed who he believed to be behind it all:

> ... The true God is a living, intelligent, powerful being.
>
> ... He governs all things and knows all things that are done or can be done.
>
> ... He endures forever and is everywhere present.
>
> ... As a blind man has no idea of colors, so we have no idea of the manner by which all wise God perceives and understands all things.[29]

Newton died in his sleep March 31, 1727, and was buried in Westminster Abbey. He left behind more than four million unpublished words. A surprising portion of those words were devoted to theology and Bible prophecy.[30]

The coexistence of science and the Bible in the lives of men like Bacon and Newton is not coincidental. The rise of science during the years that the Bible was spreading across Europe is not coincidental either. While the Bible didn't cause the scientific revolution by itself, historian Rodney Stark explains that the biblical concept of God was *necessary* for the scientific revolution:

> *Keep in mind that I am arguing only that a particular conception of a Creator was necessary for the rise of science, not that it was a sufficient cause.... Many other cultural and social developments were necessary for the rise of science ... To sum up: the rise of science was not an extension of classical [Greek] learning. It was the natural outgrowth of Christian doctrine: nature exists because it was created by God. To love and honor God, one must fully appreciate the wonders*

29. Isaac Newton, *Philosophiae Naturalis Principia Mathematica* (Florian Cajori's translation. University of California Press, 1934), 543-47.
30. Giorgio Tourne, *You Are My Witnesses: The Waldensians across Eight Hundred Years* (Cincinnati: Friendship press, 1989), 49.

of his handiwork. Moreover, because God is perfect, his handiwork functions in accord with immutable principles. But with the full use of our God-given powers of reason and observation, we ought to be able to discover these principles.[31]

The Bible also presents two concepts about "truth" that formed the basis for scientific "laws": 1) Perspicuity: Truth can be known, and 2) Immutability: Truth doesn't change. As Alfred North Whitehead (1861-1947) said in one of his lectures at Harvard in 1925:

... Without this belief the incredible labors of scientists would be without hope. It is this instinctive conviction, vividly poised before the imagination, which is the motive of power of research: – that there is a secret, a secret which can be unveiled. How has this conviction been so vividly implanted in the European mind? When we compare this tone of thought in Europe with the attitude of other civilizations when left to themselves, there seems to be but one source of its origin... the medieval insistence on the rationality of God, conceived as with the personal energy of Jehovah and with the rationality of a Greek philosopher.[32]

In other words, if men like Bacon and Newton had not believed that there was a Designer, they probably would never have gone looking for the design itself—and they learned about the Designer from their Bibles. Other factors played a part in the rise of science, for sure, but without the Bible it wouldn't have all come together in 17th-century Europe, nor would science have come to America in the early decades of that century.

31. Stark, *For the Glory of God*, 150, 157.
32. Alfred North Whitehead, *Science and the Modern World* (New York, The Free Press, 1925), 13.

Thomas Paine (1737-1809) was one of the least religious of America's founding fathers. He was a controversial theologian and philosopher among his more conservative colleagues. Nonetheless, Paine knew the Bible's worldview was inseparable from the scientific worldview. During a lecture in Paris in 1797, he criticized the French for their secular teaching of science in the public schools:

> *...With reference to the being who is the author of them: for all the principles of science are of Divine origin... When we examine an extraordinary piece of machinery, and astonishing pile of architecture, a well-executed statue or a highly finished painting... Our ideas are naturally led to think of the extensive genius and talents of the artist. When we study the elements of geometry, we think of Euclid. When we speak of gravitation, we think of Newton. How is it then that when we study the works of God in the creation, we stop short and do not think of God? It is from the error of the schools... The evil that has resulted... has been that of generating in the pupils a species of atheism. Instead of looking through the works of the creation to the creator himself, they stop short and employ the knowledge they acquire to create doubts of his existence.[33]*

During this time period in America, the Bible and science enjoyed a fairly peaceful coexistence. Much of the scientific and theological reasoning that came out of this period of time was based on a philosophy of "common sense" which said that truth is not only knowable and unchangeable, but that truth is obvious too. For example, the writers of the Declaration of Independence believed that certain truths were "self-evident" and stood alone:

33. Daniel Edwin Wheeler, ed., *Thomas Paine* (New York: Vincent Parke and Company, 1908), 2-4.

> *We hold these truths to be self-evident, that all men are created equal, that they are endowed by their Creator with certain unalienable Rights, that among these are Life, Liberty and the pursuit of Happiness.*

Another example of "common sense" is found in William Paley's (1743-1805) *Natural Theology*. Paley asked what someone would think if they found a watch in the wilderness. The logical conclusion would be to assume that someone had made the watch since something that complex could not have created itself. Then he described some of the complex biological systems that were known at the time. He concluded that the universe is like a fine watch, and that it is evidence of a watchmaker.

The same "common sense" approach was widely used for Bible interpretation as well. Many felt that the truth in the Bible could be known and that these truths didn't change. The "inductive" Bible study method, which adhered to a method of "Observation, Interpretation, and Application"—similar to the scientific method of Bacon, soon grew in popularity:

> *"Applied to biblical interpretation, the Baconian method stipulated that the first step is to free our minds from all historical theological formulation … With mind washed clean from merely human speculations, we confront the biblical text as a collection of 'facts' that speak for themselves—and then compile individual verses inductively into a theological system. Statements in Scripture were treated as analogous to facts in nature, knowable in exactly the same way…. Charles Hodge even compared the propositions in the Bible with the 'oceans, continents, islands, mountains, and rivers' studied by geography. That's why he could say, 'The Bible is to the theologian what nature is to the man of science. It is his store-house of facts."* [34]

---

34. Nancy Pearcey and Phillip E. Johnson, *Total Truth* (Wheaton: Crossway Books, 2005), 299.

In 1848, Professor Asa Mahan of Oberlin wrote that the Bible is "a scientific treaty" on reality which reveals a "universal system of moral duty."[35] Thomas Jefferson wrote:

> *Bacon, Locke and Newton... I consider them as the three greatest men that have ever lived, without any exception and as having laid the foundation of those superstructures which have been raised in the Physical and Moral sciences.*[36]

During the critical decades of America's founding, and for nearly another 100 years after, the Bible and science coexisted in a fairly peaceful and dependent marriage-like relationship. But midway through the 1800s, that relationship was seriously challenged.

THE GREAT AMERICAN DEBATE

On November 24, 1859 Charles Darwin (1809-1882) published *On the Origin of Species by Means of Natural Selection, or the Preservation of Favoured Races in the Struggle for Life*. It was certainly not the first time that someone had proposed a theory for the gradual development of life over time by natural processes, but Darwin's theory gained fairly wide readership and acceptance in a short period of time.

The conflict between the biblical account of creation and Darwin's theory of evolution forced some to make critical decisions about what they believed. Some began to lean on personal experience and feeling as truth, disregarding what the Bible *or* science says, and instead allowing their emotions and knowledge to decide what is right. Others carefully weighed the evidence of both science and Scripture. Then, they tried to reconcile evolution

---

35. Asa Mahan, *A Science of Moral Philosophy* (Oberlin Archives, 1848), 187,183.
36. *"The Letters of Thomas Jefferson: 1743–1826 Bacon, Locke, and Newton,"* accessed July 28, 2012, http://www.let.rug.nl/usa/P/tj3/writings/brf/jefl74.htm.

and creation with each other, attempting to give credence to the idea that perhaps they are both true... somehow. Still others began to separate out scientific truths from spiritual truth in their own minds—thinking spiritually on Sunday, but secularly at home, school, and at work. However people responded, it seemed that a formal separation between science and the Bible had begun with no chance of uniting the two again.

That perception continues today. In 2005, Gallup[37] asked:

Which comes closer to your view about the relationship between science and religion?

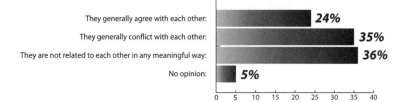

If Darwin signaled the beginning of the marital separation of science and the Bible, the great divorce between them in America took place 60 years later. In 1925, John W. Butler, a Tennessee State Representative and head of the World Christian Fundamentals Association, pushed for an anti-evolution law, forbidding the teaching of evolution in public schools. The American Civil Liberties Union responded by recruiting John Scopes, a substitute biology teacher, to test the law.

Scopes was charged on May 5, 1925 with teaching evolution. When reporters flooded the town of Dayton, Tennessee, for the trial, a media frenzy exploded. The proceedings were broadcast through live radio and printed in daily newspaper headlines coast to coast. The Bible became a central focus of the conflict on the seventh day of the trial, when the prosecution and

---

37. *"Evolution, Creationism, Intelligent Design,"* The Gallup Organization, accessed March 24, 2012, http://www.gallup.com/poll/21814/evolution-creationism-intelligent-design.aspx.

defense exchanged jabs. The proceedings quickly escalated into a national publicity spectacle that exposed the apparently intense incompatibilities between the Bible and science and the irreconcilable differences between the fact-driven secular scientists and the faith-based clergy.

A line had been drawn between the two. As science continued to accelerate into the future, the Bible appeared to be a relic from the past. Darwin and Scopes had sent the Bible and science in different directions ... and science appeared to be winning the custody suit for the heart of America.

During the decades since Scopes, many have made bold predictions about the death of God, religion and the Bible. F.C. Wallace, in a popular undergraduate college textbook, wrote:

> *The evolutionary future of religion is extinction. Belief in supernatural beings and in supernatural forces that affect nature without obeying nature's laws will erode and become only an interesting memory.... Belief in supernatural powers is doomed to die out, all over the world, as a result of the increasing adequacy and diffusion of scientific knowledge.... The process is inevitable.*[38]

The universe was now being explained by the laws of physics alone. Astronomer and atheist Carl Sagan said there was "nothing for a Creator to do" and every thinking person was therefore forced to admit "the absence of God."[39] Richard Dawkins, a famous scientist, boldly proclaimed in the *New York Times* in 1989:

> *It is absolutely safe to say that, if you meet somebody who claims not to believe in evolution, that person is ignorant, stupid, or insane (or wicked, but I'd rather not*

---

38. Anthony F. C. Wallace, *Religion: An Anthropological View* (New York: Random House, 1966), 264-65.
39. Sharon Begley, *"Science Finds God,"* Newsweek, July 20, 1989, 44.
40. Richard Dawkins, *"Ignorance Is No Crime."* Free Inquiry Magazine, Volume 21, Number 3. www.secularhumanism.org.

consider that).[40]

Science and the Bible had parted ways. Faith and fact were now clearly divorced and reconciliation was no longer an option. Furthermore, in the hearts and minds of many Americans, atheistic science was clearly triumphing over the Bible.

Or was it?

WHAT AMERICANS BELIEVE

One of the core elements of the scientific method is the "hypothesis." A scientific hypothesis is an untested claim that can be tested to be shown false. When a so called authority like Wallace hypothesizes that "belief in supernatural powers is doomed to die out" or when Dawkins asserts that a creationist is "ignorant, stupid, or insane," it seems logical to test such statements with measurable facts. What do Americans believe about the Bible and science? Scientific surveys paint a very different picture than the scenario that the outspoken secular scientists and philosophers predicted. For example, in September of 2005, Gallup asked:

Which of the following statements comes closest to your views on the origin and development of human beings?[41]

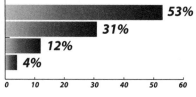

In America today, only 12% accept the purely atheistic theory of evolution. The majority, at 53%, believe the Bible's account of human origins. Nearly a third believes that God guided a linear progression of the complexity of life that resulted in humans. Add that together and a full 84% believe God was involved in

---

37. *"Evolution, Creationism, Intelligent Design,"* The Gallup Organization, accessed March 24, 2012, http://www.gallup.com/poll/21814/evolution-creationism-intelligent-design.aspx.

some way. No, God is not dead in the American mind; not by a long shot!

The survey we did through America's Research Group in 2010 asked the question differently: *Do you believe in biblical creation where God created Adam and Eve as the first man and woman?*

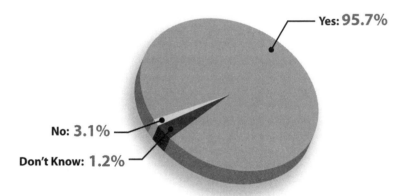

Yes: **95.7%**

No: **3.1%**

Don't Know: **1.2%**

Those are stunning results, actually. Evolution has dominated education and the media over the last half century. A full generation has grown up with "evolution only" public education. Why would so many of us continue to believe in the Bible and God?

First, biology has revealed that life is far more complicated than was initially believed. In his groundbreaking work, *Origin of the Species*, Darwin said:

> *If it could be demonstrated that any complex organ existed which could not possibly have been formed by numerous, successive, slight modifications, my theory would absolutely break down.*

Since Darwin, the unthinkably complex processes of a simple cell have been revealed—including the discovery of DNA, a biological informational structure that must exist *before* a cell could ever exist. Also, *all* organs (such as the eye or kidney) have turned out to be *incredibly* complex. Science is giving us an ever-increasingly detailed view of life that is *exponentially* more complicated than anything Darwin could imagine. The scientific field of biochemistry, for example, didn't even really exist until the mid-1900s. Biochemistry has revealed a stunning number of intricately complex biological systems "which could not possibly have been formed by numerous, successive, slight modifications..." as Darwin knew his theory required.[42]

Second, paleontology (the study of fossils) has not produced the trail of evidence earlier scientists thought it would. Darwin himself asked a probing question in *Origin of the Species*, Chapter VI-Difficulties on Theory:

> *Why, if species have descended from other species by fine graduations, do we not everywhere see innumerable transitional forms? Why is not all nature in confusion instead of the species being, as we see them, well-defined?*

His answer to his own questions was reasonable. In the late 1800s, paleontology was in its infancy. Darwin believed that just because transitional forms had not been found *yet*, they would be in the future. Others hypothesized that new species might have evolved in just a small area during a short period of time, and then spread out across the world *without* evolving further, thus showing up throughout the fossil record as complete forms. The last 100+ years of fossil discovery and research, however, shows that species in the fossil record are still "well-defined" and not "in confusion" as they would be if life was continually evolving.

The science of mathematics has also shed light on the probabilities of basic life coming into being by random chance. Atheist Fred Hoyle (writing with Chandra Wickramasinghe) calculated that the odds of obtaining just the enzymes for a simple

---

42. For a compelling analysis of the complexity of human biochemistry, see Michael Behe, *Darwin's Black Box: The Biochemical Challenge to Evolution* (Free Press, 1996).

cell by random chance are 1 to $10^{40,000}$ (and there are only about 10^{80} atoms in the whole universe). He admitted that the formation of a simple cell by chance is comparable to the likelihood of a tornado blowing through a junkyard and assembling a 747.[43]

So, not only did science fail to drive the Bible into "extinction," but it appears to be having the opposite effect. In July of 1998, *Newsweek* ran an article entitled "Science Finds God," which quoted many leading scientists who found faith in the midst of scientific fact:

> *"When you realize that the laws of nature must be incredibly finely tuned to produce the universe we see," says John Polkinghorne, who had a distinguished career as a physicist at Cambridge University before becoming an Anglican priest in 1982, "that conspires to plant the idea that the universe did not just happen, but that there must be a purpose behind it."... Charles Townes, who shared the 1964 Nobel Prize in Physics for discovering the principles of the laser, goes further: "Many have a feeling that somehow intelligence must have been involved in the laws of the universe."[44]*

SCOPES REVISITED

It should now come as no surprise that Americans believe that the Bible and science are compatible, even though a few leading spokespersons would like us to believe otherwise. The 2005 study by Gallup asked two questions that shed interesting light on how public opinion would view the Scopes Monkey Trial today:

If the public schools in your community taught the theory of evolution,—that is, the idea that human beings evolved from other species of animals—would you be upset, or not?[45]

---

43. *"Hoyle on Evolution,"* Nature, Vol. 294, November 12, 1981, 105.
44. Sharon Begley, *"Science Finds God,"* 45.
45. *"Evolution, Creationism, Intelligent Design,"* The Gallup Organization, accessed March 24, 2012, http://www.gallup.com/poll/21814/evolution-creationism-intelligent-design.aspx.

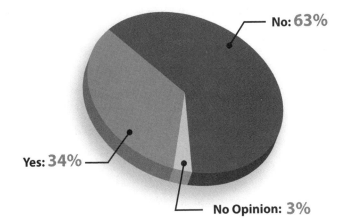

No: 63%

Yes: 34%

No Opinion: 3%

If the public schools in your community taught the theory of creationism—that is, the idea that human beings were created by God in their present form and did not evolve from other species of animals—would you be upset, or not?

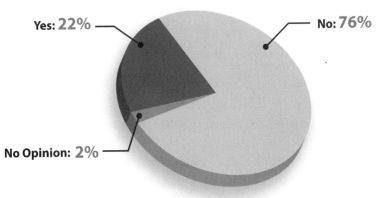

Yes: 22%

No: 76%

No Opinion: 2%

By analyzing how people answered both of these questions, Gallup calculated that 30% would be upset if *only* evolution were taught. Far fewer (18%) would be upset if creationism were taught but not evolution. Significantly, only 4% of Americans would be upset if *both* evolution and creation were taught. It would appear that Americans are not afraid to learn about things that we might not agree with—but we don't like it when someone else filters out which theories we are exposed to. We want to know the scientific evidence that supports creationism. We want to know the problems with evolutionary theory. The vast majority of us want to know it all. When it comes to the Bible and science, we prefer to get all the facts so that we can make our own decisions about what we will believe.

THE DEATH OF GOD?

On April 8, 1966, *Time* magazine's cover asked in bold red letters, "Is God Dead?" It was an honest question. Many felt that science and philosophy had not only triumphed over faith, but that they had killed the concept of God entirely. Philosopher Frederick Nietzsche claimed that all of us were responsible:

> *God is dead. God remains dead. And we have killed him. How shall we comfort ourselves, the murderers of all murderers? What was holiest and mightiest of all that the world has yet owned has bled to death under our knives: who will wipe this blood off us? What water is there for us to clean ourselves? What festivals of atonement, what sacred games shall we have to invent? Is not the greatness of this deed too great for us? Must we ourselves not become gods simply to appear worthy of it?*[46]

Once again, the Bible appeared to have been run over by the freight train of modern thinking. The Bible and the biblical concept of God, we were told, were only old-fashioned residue from the past; they had been killed and buried for good. But is that what happened? In the book *What Americans Really Believe*, Rodney Stark called this claim "The Godless Revolution That

---

46. Frederick Nietzsche, *The Gay Science*, Section 125, 1882 (New York: Vintage Books, 1974) translated by Walter Kaufmann.

Never Happened." Using data from numerous sources, Stark clearly shows that those who believe that God is dead in the American heart are clearly mistaken.

Percent of Those Who Do Not Believe in God by Year:

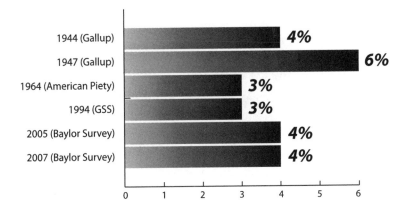

A 2005 Gallup survey asked for more detail[47]:

Which one statement comes closest to your personal beliefs about God?

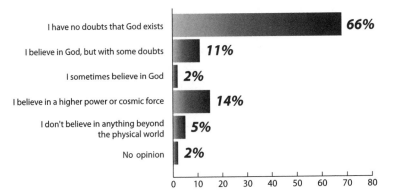

Again, the percentages here are decisive. God is alive and well in this country, and there seems to be plenty of room for doubters

---

47. *"The Values and Beliefs of the American Public, A National Study,"* The Gallup Organization, 2005.

and for those who do not believe in the traditional concept of God. Only those who don't believe in anything are in the obvious minority. Beyond that, surveys show that Americans have a high level of belief in things the Bible says exist:

In your opinion, does each of the following exist?

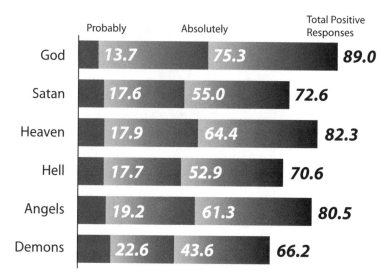

Americans also feel that God cares about them personally. When asked if they believe that God is "concerned with my personal well-being," 45% "strongly agree" and 30% "agree," for a total over 70%. The vast majority of Americans also believe what the Bible says about Jesus:

> Which one statement comes closest to your personal beliefs about Jesus?
>
> - 1 %: Jesus is a fictional character.
>
> - 3.3 %: Jesus probably existed, but he was not special.
>
> - 8 %: Jesus was an extraordinary person, but he was not a messenger of God.

- 12.2 %: Jesus was one of many messengers or prophets of God.

- 70.9 %: Jesus is the son of God.

- 4.6 %: No opinion

Even "controversial" ancient historical events show a high level of belief. Our 2010 America's Research Group study asked:

Do you believe in a worldwide global flood where only Noah and those in the ark survived the flood?

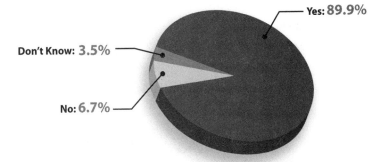

Darwin and Scopes may have given the *impression* that science and the Bible have irreconcilable differences, but most Americans have no problem *integrating* the two. In 2005 Gallup surveyed 1,600 people. In the survey, Gallup asked the following:

Please indicate your level of agreement with the following statements about science:

Science and religion are incompatible.[48]

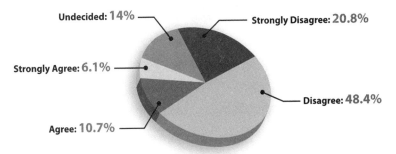

48. *"Evolution, Creationism, Intelligent Design,"* The Gallup Organization, accessed March 24, 2012, http://www.gallup.com/poll/21814/evolution-creationism-intelligent-design.aspx.

Simply stated, nearly 70% of Americans *disagree* that science and religion are incompatible.

The 2010 Barna study with ABS[49] showed that Americans disagree with other assumptions often made about the Bible:

- Six out of every ten adults (61%) strongly disagree with the statement "the Bible is not credible or trustworthy," compared to only 8% who strongly agree.

- The majority (54%) also strongly reject the concept that the Bible is not relevant to their life, while one in nine (11%) are in strong agreement.

- A similar proportion (53%) also strongly disagree that the Bible is boring, with only 6% in strong agreement with that particular description.

It *looked* like the 1900s were the end of the beautiful union that science and the Bible experienced in the earlier decades of America, but that's just not the case. Scientifically conducted surveys prove differently. We still define ourselves by our belief in the Bible in the modern world.

How well does the term "Bible believing" describe your religious identity?[50]

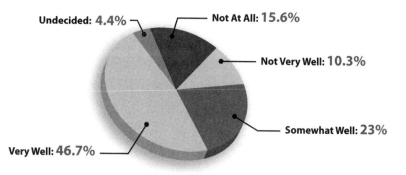

Undecided: 4.4%

Not At All: 15.6%

Not Very Well: 10.3%

Somewhat Well: 23%

Very Well: 46.7%

49. American Bible Society, The Barna Group, *The State of the Bible 2011* (New York, NY, 2011), 7.
50. *"The Values and Beliefs of the American Public: A National Study,"* The Gallup Organization, 2007.

Some may be using science as a haven for atheistic beliefs, but the vast majority of Americans see science and faith as compatible. Furthermore, most Americans identify themselves as Bible believers. Overall, we believe foundational Bible teachings about spiritual beings and places (even though those things are outside of the scope of true scientific investigation). In fact, two-thirds of us would say "Bible believing" describes us "well."

History and the statistics indicate America, the Bible and science have enjoyed a powerful and positive relationship with each other from the very beginning. That healthy relationship continues today... and that relationship is not likely to dissolve.

SCIENCE IMPACTING THE BIBLE TODAY AND TOMORROW

Gutenberg's printing press was revolutionary in the 1600s, but new technologies absolutely dwarf its capabilities in the 21st century. Innovations in digital print-on-demand technologies will soon make hard copies of the Bible available on every continent, in thousands of languages, for a price of about a dollar each.

The tools of science are being used to research the Bible as never before. The Center for the Study of New Testament Manuscripts, for example, is traveling the globe making high-resolution digital images of tens of thousands of important Bibles and manuscripts and then making them available to the public online. *(www.CSNTM.org)*. Just a few years ago, scholars were rarely able to work with physical manuscripts. They had to work from microfilm images, which were expensive, cumbersome, and hard to get. The availability of these new images is giving researchers unparalleled access to documents that can be scrutinized to confirm and improve the accuracy of the Bibles we

These images show the difference between microfilm and high-resolution digital images.

read today.

Other technologies are shedding new light on ancient manuscripts, literally. Dr. Dirk Obbink from Oxford oversees the research of manuscripts that were found in the ancient dump of Oxyrynchus, a city on a tributary of the Nile River. This single cache has been under study for over a hundred years—yet hundreds of tin containers have yet to be opened. Recently, Dr. Obbink and his team developed new technologies for reading text that is severely faded. He and his team have even been able to decipher text which has been covered over by plaster or other text. Dirk explains the technology this way:

> *Multi spectral imaging takes images at the different levels of the light spectrum, from ultraviolet to infrared, and then sandwiches them together into a composite image to see what the naked eye cannot see. The process is capable of picking up inks which lie deeply embedded into the fabric of the papyri and contrasting them with the only slightly darker surface around them. The process has been extended further to be able to read the papyri that were recycled into papier-mâché-like decorative funeral art that the Greeks and the Romans placed over mummies. What we have discovered is that the multi spectral imaging can see through that thin layer of plaster and reveal the written layer of writing underneath without having to dissolve the painted surface on the mummy. We have also been able to apply the technique to medieval manuscripts. The thin animal skins were commonly scraped off and washed for reuse. Multi-spectral imaging allows us to actually see the erased text.*

The Bible claims to be God's Word, and most Americans believe that it is. Throughout the centuries, critics have hypothesized that the Bible was written long after the events it claims to report, and many have theorized that the Bible is full of errors. We should never run from such scrutiny. We should search everything to find out the truth *about* the Bible to discover the truth *within* the Bible. Now, through various facets of science, those hypotheses can be tested at levels never before possible including:

- Multi-Spectral Imaging surface analysis
- Hair follicle analysis
- Chemical analysis of the surface
- Chemical analysis of the composition of the inks

These *are* unprecedented times. The relationship between the Bible and science is building on the past and moving ahead in ways we never could have imagined or believed only a few decades ago. The Bible was integral to the birth of science. Together, they shaped the modern Western world. Now they move ahead together into the future, continuing to bring fact and faith together.

Four:

The BIBLE *in* EDUCATION

"If a man is not familiar with the Bible, he has suffered the loss which he had better make all possible haste to correct.... A thorough knowledge of the Bible is worth more than a college education."— Teddy Roosevelt[51]

For the past 400 years, the American educational system has become instrumental in defining who we are. It is central to our society, shapes generation after generation, and has been the envy of the world. America not only educates its own citizens, we educate more foreign students than any other country. About 700,000 foreign students (one-third of all the world's students who are studying abroad) have come here in search of knowledge in a country that strives for equality, free speech, innovation, and academic excellence. Many of our forefathers came here for the same reason. While the future superiority of our education system is uncertain, the past success is easily verified.

---

51. Theodore Roosevelt, *Ladies Home Journal*, October 1917, 12.

The Bible is not only the most important book in our history; it's the most important text in the history of our educational system. But its early prominence was not without controversy. From the beginning, the Bible has generated passionate debate with a massive amount of legal scrutiny and deep consideration of constitutional issues. The debates continue today as the Bible appears on the covers of national newsmagazines, is debated in town hall meetings, and becomes an issue in election campaigns locally and nationally. What is the history of the Bible in American education? How do we feel about it today? What does the future look like?

THE HEART OF THE IVY LEAGUE

Harvard University was founded in 1636, making it our oldest institution of higher learning. Its early graduates included John Hancock, Samuel Adams, John Adams, and Fisher Ames— men who went on to be key players in our nation's history. From the beginning, Harvard instituted principles that would establish it as one of the most respected universities in the world. One of its educational practices made it clear that the Bible would play a major role, not only in the philosophy of the institution as a whole, but in the lives of all attendees; "Everyone shall so exercise himself in reading the Scriptures twice a day that he shall be ready to give such an account of his proficiency therein."[52] President John Quincy Adams also served as a Harvard professor. He said:

> With regard to the history contained in the Bible... It is not so much praiseworthy to be acquainted with it as it is shameful to be ignorant of it.[53]

---

52. Benjamin Pierce, *A History of Harvard University* (Reprint, Kessinger Publishing, 2010), Appendix, page 5.
53. John Quincy Adams, *Letters of John Quincy Adams to His Son on the Bible and Its Teachings* (Auburn: James M. Alden, 1850), 34.

Statue in front of Harvard Chapel shows John Harvard (1607-1608) reading his Bible.

Yale was founded in 1701 as a training center for clergy and political leaders. It was also one of the key ignition points for the American Revolution. Several signers of the Declaration of Independence (such as Lyman Hall and Philip Livingston) studied there. Some Yale students went on to sign the Constitution, such as Abraham Baldwin and William Livingston. Other leaders from Yale include James Kent, who was called "the Father of American Jurisprudence," and Zephaniah Swift, who wrote the first American legal textbook. The Bible had an influence not only on this institution, but on most of its students. As part of its requirements for attendance, Article 1 and 4 of Chapter II in *The Laws of Yale College* stipulated:

> *All the scholars are required to live a religious and blameless life according to the rules of God's Word, diligently reading the Holy Scriptures… and constantly attending to all the duties of religion.*[54]

54. *The Laws of Yale College in New Haven in Connecticut* (New Haven: Josiah Meigs, 1789), 5-6, Chapter II, Article 1, 4.

Princeton was also started as a ministerial training school. The same is true of Dartmouth, which was opened as a mission training school for Native Americans and those of European descent. Dartmouth's motto is *Vox Clamantis in Deserto*, a phrase which appeared five times in the Latin Vulgate Bible meaning "the voice of one crying in the wilderness." This reference remains on Dartmouth's seal today.

Even in state universities, the Bible was once a part of regular life. A survey of state universities conducted by James Angell (President of the University of Vermont and the University of Michigan) found that in 1890, 90% of the schools held their own chapel services (50% of which were mandatory). In addition, Angell's survey revealed that 25% of the schools required church attendance.

CLASSROOMS, CONGRESS, AND COURTS

From the earliest of days, the Bible permeated every level of American education. Many of these early settlers had been the victims of religious persecution and had come here in search of religious freedom. They were also aware of the atrocities that had occurred in the name of Christianity in Europe (like the Crusades and the Spanish Inquisition). These freedom seekers believed that Americans needed to be literate, so that they could read the Bible for themselves and not be deceived by "evil forces" and corrupt leaders. In response to these concerns, the first public education law was enacted in 1647, requiring every town with 50 or more households to appoint a teacher for reading and writing. The wording of the law explains the motivation:

> *It being one chief project of that old deluder, Satan, to*
> *keep men from the knowledge of the Scriptures, as in*

former times by keeping them in an unknown tongue,
so in these latter times by persuading from the use of
tongues, so that at least the true sense and meaning
of the original might be clouded and corrupted with
false glosses of saint-seeming deceivers; and to the end
that learning may not be buried in the grave of our
forefathers, in church and commonwealth, the Lord
assisting our endeavors.[55]

By the late 1600s, some civil leaders were concerned that many children were still illiterate. The reason for this concern was evident in the 1690 Connecticut Illiteracy Law, which was enacted to help fix the problem:

This (legislature) observing that notwithstanding our
former orders made for the education of children...
There are many persons unable to read the English
tongue, and thereby incapable of reading the holy word
of God or the good laws of this (state).

On the federal level, The Northwest Ordinance contained the first law dealing with education. It was passed by the same founding fathers who drafted the First Amendment. Signed by President George Washington, article III says:

Religion, morality, and knowledge, being necessary to
good government and the happiness of mankind, schools
and the means of education shall be forever encouraged.[56]

Noah Webster had a major impact on American education. He was a legislator and a judge who worked with the Founding

---

55. *Records of the Governor and Company of the Massachusetts Bay in New England* (1853), II: 203.
56. *The Constitution of the United States of America with the Latest Amendments* (Trenton: Morre and Lake, 1813), 364. *"An Ordinance of the Territory of the United States Northwest of the River Ohio,"* Article III.

Fathers on the final wording of the Constitution. He authored numerous textbooks, helped found Amherst College, and was given the honorific title "The Schoolmaster to America."

His dictionary defined 70,000 words. Twelve thousand of those words had never appeared in another dictionary. It took him two decades to complete the massive two-volume work. He traveled extensively, becoming familiar with more than 20 languages, allowing him to trace the foreign roots of thousands of English words. Webster regularly used Bible quotes in his textbooks and dictionary. In defining "man," for example, he quoted Genesis 1:26, Job 14:1, 1 Corinthians 10:13 and Matthew 4:4. These references were removed from Webster's dictionary after his death, but the Bible's influence on his life, his writing, and his views toward America cannot be erased. In his book, *History of the United States,* he states:

> *The brief exposition of the Constitution of the United States will unfold to young persons the principles of Republican government.... Our citizens should early understand that the genuine source of correct Republican principles is the Bible-particularly the New Testament....*[57]

Benjamin Rush (1746-1813) was an early influential American educator. He signed the Declaration of Independence, wrote America's first chemistry book and was called "The Father of American Medicine." He was one of the first Founding Fathers to propose a nationwide public school system, also earning him the title "The Father of Public Schools under the Constitution." Rush started five different colleges, three of which are still open today: Dickenson College, Franklin College (now Franklin and

---

57. Noah Webster, *History of the United States* (New Haven: Durrie & Peck, 1832), 6.

Marshal), and the College of Physicians of Philadelphia, often called the "Birthplace of American Medicine." As an aggressive advocate for human equality, he helped found the first abolition society, and was a strong proponent of education for African-Americans and women. One of Rush's many publications is entitled *A Defense of the Use of the Bible in Schools*. In this essay he states:

> *Now the Bible contains more truth than any other book in the world; so true is the testimony that it bears of God in His works of creation, providence, and redemption that it is called truth itself, by way of preeminence above other things that are acknowledged to be true. How forcibly are we struck with the evidence of truth in the history of the Jews, above what we discover in the history of other nations. Where do we find a hero of a historian record his own faults and vices except in the Old Testament? Indeed, my friend, from some accounts which I have read of the American Revolution, I begin to grow skeptical to all history except that which is contained in the Bible. Now, if this book be known to contain nothing but what is materially true, the mind will naturally acquire a love for it from this circumstance; and from this affection for the truths of the Bible, it will acquire a discernment of truth in other books, and a reference of it in all the transactions of life. Of how much consequence, then, must it be to fill the mind with that species of knowledge in childhood and youth which, when recalled in the decline of life, will support the soul under the infirmities of age and smooth the avenues of approaching death....*

Benjamin Rush, "The Father of Public Schools under the Constitution."

In the same essay Dr. Rush proclaims,

> *We err, not only in human affairs but in religion likewise, only because we do not know the Scriptures and obey their instructions. Immense truths, I believe, are concealed in them. The time, I have no doubt, will come when posterity will view and pity our ignorance of these truths.... In contemplating the political institutions of this United States, I lament that we waste so much time and money in punishing crimes and take so little pains to prevent them.... For this divine book, above all others, favors that equality among mankind, the respect for just laws, and those sober and frugal virtues which constitute the soul of (our government).*

Another Founding Father demonstrating strong biblical beliefs in education was Fisher Ames (1758-1808), a Congressman from Massachusetts. During the First Session of the Congress (when the Bill of Rights was created), he proposed the final wording for the First Amendment, which passed the U.S. House of Representatives in 1789. It reads:

Congress shall make no law respecting an establishment of religion, or prohibiting the free exercise thereof; or abridging the freedom of speech, or of the press; or the right of the people peaceably to assemble, and to petition the Government for a redress of grievances.

Congressman Fisher Ames

As more textbooks became available, Ames had a growing concern about a trend he saw in American education. On September 20, 1789, in an article published in *Palladium* magazine, he wrote:

We have a dangerous trend beginning to take place in our education. We're starting to put more and more textbooks into our schools… We are spending less time in the classroom in the Bible, which should be the principle text in our schools…. The Bible states these great moral lessons better than any other manmade book.

He wrote again of his concerns in 1801:

> *It has been the custom of late years to put a number*
> *of little books into the hands of children, containing*
> *fables and moral lessons. This is very well, because it is*
> *right, first to raise curiosity and then to guide it.... Why*
> *then, if these books for children must be retained, as they*
> *will be, should not the Bible regain the place it once*
> *held as a school-book? Its morals are pure, its examples*
> *captivating and noble. The reverence for the sacred book,*
> *that is thus early impressed, lasts long - and probably, if*
> *not impressed in infancy never takes firm hold of the*
> *mind. One consideration more is important: In no book*
> *is there so good english [sic], so pure and so elegant - and*
> *by teaching all the same book they will speak alike, and*
> *the bible will justly remain the standard of language as*
> *well as of faith. A barbarous provincial jargon will be*
> *banished, and taste, corrupted by pompous Johnsonian*
> *affectation, will be restored.*

While his writings about the Bible are lesser known, Ames'
wording in the First Amendment continues to be the flash-point
of debate regarding the role of the Bible in schools today. What do
we, as Americans, now believe about teaching the Bible in public
education? A CBS News opinion poll in February of 2009[58] shows
division on the issue.

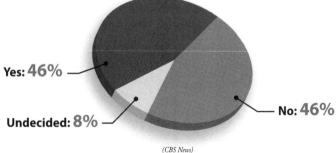

(CBS News)

58. Joel Roberts, *"Split over Bibles in Schools."* CBS News.http://www.cbsnews.com/stories/2006/04/14/opinion/
polls/main1500906.shtml.

Interestingly, about half of Americans believe that teaching the Bible in public schools is a violation of the First Amendment. It appears that 46% of Americans interpret the phrase "Congress shall make no law respecting an establishment of religion" to mean that there must be a complete "separation of church and state" (a phrase which doesn't appear in the Constitution). Many of us who adhere to this idea feel that anything religious must be removed from the public arena, including the Bible.

The other half of us believes that the First Amendment was written to keep the government from *legislating* religion or *creating* a state-sponsored religion—that is, that the government needs to stay out of religion, but religion (including a religious book such as the Bible) is allowed in the public arena. This would be the logical conclusion based on Ames' writings about both topics.

THE NEW ENGLAND PRIMER

14   NEW ENGLAND PRIMER.

Time cuts down all
Both great and small

Uriah's beauteous wife
Made David seek his life.

Whales in the sea
God's voice obey,

Xerxes the Great did die,
And so must you and I.

Youth forward slips,
Death soonest nips.

Zaccheus, he
Did climb the tree,
His Lord to see.

T U V W X Y Z

NEW ENGLAND PRIMER.   15

AN ALPHABET OF LESSONS FOR CHILDREN.

A WISE son makes a glad father, but a foolish son is the heaviness of his mother.

BETTER is a little, with the fear of the Lord, than great treasure, and trouble therewith.

COME unto Christ, all ye who labor and are heavy laden, and he will give you rest.

DO not the abominable thing which I hate, saith the Lord.

EXCEPT a man be born again, he cannot see the kingdom of God.

FOOLISHNESS is bound up in the heart of a child, but the rod of correction will drive it from him.

GRIEVE not the Holy Spirit, lest it depart from thee.

HOLINESS becomes God's house forever.

IT is good for me to draw near unto God.

KEEP thy heart with all diligence, for out of it are the issues of life.

LIARS will have their part in the lake which burns with fire and brimstone.

The New England Primer was America's first textbook. First printed in 1690 in Boston, it was used for two hundred years in America's schools and became *the* reading and writing textbook of American education. Benjamin Franklin, Samuel Adams, and Noah Webster had the textbook reprinted for their generation. It influenced students well into the 20th century and is still available today.[59] The influence of the Bible in the text is evident from beginning to end.

> The alphabet was taught using Biblical examples:
>
> A – *A wise son makes a glad father, but a foolish son is the heaviness of his mother.*
>
> B – *Better is little with fear of the Lord than great treasure and trouble therewith.*
>
> C – *Come unto Christ ye that labor and are heavy laden and He will give you rest.*
>
> D – *Do not the abominable thing which I hate saith the Lord.*
>
> E – *Except a man be born again, he cannot see the Kingdom of God.*

Prayers, creeds, and hymns were used as texts for reading. The final letter of John Rogers (which was written to his children only days before he was burned at the stake by Queen Mary) was included as a message of advice to students (and, perhaps, as a reminder of the religious freedom they now enjoyed in America). The 107 questions of the Westminster Catechism taught basic theology. The first two questions were:

> Q: 1. What is the chief end of man?
>
> A: Man's chief end is to glorify God and enjoy him forever.

---

59. For a copy of the *New England Primer*, contact Wall Builders, at 800-873-2845 or www.wallbuilders.com.

Q: 2.   What rule hath God given to direct us how
        we may glorify and enjoy him?

A: The word of God which is contained in
        the Scriptures of the Old and New Testament
        is the only rule to direct us how we may
        glorify God and enjoy him.

A Short Prayer to be Used Every Morning is included in the
back of the 1805 edition:

> *O Lord, our heavenly Father, almighty and everlasting*
> *God. I most humbly thank thee for thy great mercy and*
> *goodness in preserving and keeping me from all perils*
> *and dangers of this night past, and bringing me safely*
> *in the beginning of this day; defend me, O Lord, in*
> *the same, with thy mighty power; and grant, that this*
> *day I may fall into no sin, neither run into danger, but*
> *that all my doings may be ordered by thy governance, to*
> *do always that which is righteous in thy sight, through*
> *Jesus Christ our Lord.*
> *Amen.*

At just three inches wide and five inches tall, the 100 pages of
the little New England Primer made a huge impact on America.
It is certainly the most widely used and long-lived textbook in our
history.

THE BEGINNING OF TODAY'S DEBATE

As the use of other textbooks increased in the early 1800s,
the use of Bible and other religious materials diminished. The
year 1827 would prove to be a turning point, when a law passed
in Massachusetts prohibiting books that promoted a particular
religion or denomination. The idea was to create a religious
"neutral zone," where no particular religion would be promoted.

Massachusetts formed a state board of education and appointed Horace Mann as president. Mann was committed to keeping religious doctrine out of the classroom. But he also wanted to keep the Bible in the schools and have it read in a way that allowed it to "speak for itself" without promoting any particular religion or denomination.[60] Then, in 1835, a revised version of the law passed which banned sectarian religious materials.

The debate had begun in earnest. Books that promoted a specific religious point of view were being eliminated from the classroom. Other states soon followed Massachusetts, and by the beginning of the Civil War, the amount of religious material in American classrooms had diminished significantly. Could the Bible remain as a neutral spiritual influence? Most people believed that it could, but the debate continued.

Daniel Webster (1782-1852) found himself in the center of the controversy in 1844. Webster was a second-generation American statesman who had been a young man during the revolution. He served several terms in the United States House of Representatives and nearly 20 years in the Senate. Some considered him to be the greatest attorney in his generation. In 1844, he argued a case before the Supreme Court dealing with a public school in Philadelphia that had forbidden ministers to visit campus. Webster presented his case for three full days, and his final day's arguments were extensively supported by quotes taken from the Bible. Justice Joseph Story wrote the unanimous decision for the Supreme Court:

> *Why may not the Bible, and especially the New Testament, without note or comment, be read and taught as Divine revelation in the (school)—its general precepts expounded... and its glorious principles of morality inculcated?... Where can the purest principles of morality be learned so clearly or so perfectly as*

---

60. Paul Gutjahr, *American Bible* (Stanford, CA: Stanford University Press, 1999), 119-120.

from the New Testament? Where are benevolence, the
love of truth, sobriety, and industry so powerfully and
irresistibly inculcated as in the sacred volume?[61]

Senator Daniel Webster

This ruling stood for over a century. For example, Justice
Robert Jackson's concurring opinion in the 1948 case *McCollum
v. Board of Education* states, "One can hardly respect the system
of education that would leave the student wholly ignorant of the
currents of religious thought that move the world society...."
Jackson warned that making God off limits in the classroom would
leave the education system "in shreds," but the momentum was
on the side of the secularists. A series of Supreme Court decisions
culminated in 1963. The decision of the *Court in Abington
Township School District v. Schempp* effectively removed prayer
and religious devotion from the classroom, beginning a new era
of secular education in America. Recent court decisions have
ordered the Bible out of school libraries in Colorado (*Roberts versus
Madigan*, 1989). In Nebraska, students have been disciplined for
bringing their personal Bibles to read during free time (*Gireke v.*

---

61. *Vidal v. Girard's Executors*, 43 U.S. 126 (1844).

Boltzer, 1989). Decades after the Abington v. Schempp decision, many school administrators (who are wary of potential lawsuits) have eliminated almost anything that could even be considered religious.

How do we, as Americans, feel about this decision? According to the 2011 ARG survey, 80% of us are "very" or "somewhat" bothered by these developments:

How much are you bothered that the courts have barred the reading of the Bible in public schools?

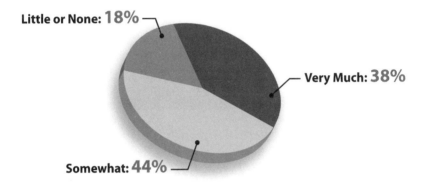

The Gallup Organization now calls us "a nation of biblical illiterates." According to one of its recent surveys, only half of U.S. adults could name even one of the Gospels. Most can't name Genesis, the Bible's first book. On March 14, 2007, *USA Today* reported that "Americans get an "F" in religion." According to that article, 60% of Americans can't name five of the Ten Commandments and 50% of high school seniors think Sodom and Gomorrah were married.

The debate continues, of course. Some surveys show that at least 60% of Americans would like to see the Bible taught in public schools again. But under the current laws, can it be done legally? The answer is "Yes" and "No." It depends on whether students are taught *about* the Bible or *from* the Bible.

In the 1963 *Schempp* decision, Justice Arthur Goldberg distinguished between "the teaching of religion" and "teaching about religion." Justice Tom C. Clark wrote, "Nothing we have said here indicates that such study of the Bible or of religion, when presented objectively as part of a secular program of education, may not be effected consistently with the First Amendment."

Most of us are unaware of this provision that allows the Bible to be taught "objectively as part of a secular program." A 2010 survey by Pew Research Center's Forum on Religion and Public Life found:

- 89% know that a teacher cannot lead his or her class in prayer.

- Only 23% know that a teacher can read from the Bible as an example of literature.

- Only 36% know that a teacher can offer a class in comparative religions.

General Counsel for the American Jewish Congress, Marc Stern, is convinced that it is "beyond question that it is possible to teach a course about the Bible that is constitutional."[62] Legal challenges today tend to focus on whether or not a course is being taught in a neutral way—and "neutral" is not always black and white. In order to clarify what is acceptable, Charles Haynes, a Senior Scholar at the First Amendment Center in Arlington, Virginia, wrote *The Bible and Public Schools: A First Amendment Guide.* These guidelines are endorsed by numerous organizations including the American Jewish Committee, the People for the American Way, the Council on Islamic Education, and the National Association of Evangelicals. These guidelines help bring clarity to those who wish to see the Bible's influence remain in the schools without compromising current legislation.

---

62. David Van Biema, *"The Case for Teaching the Bible."* Time, March 22, 2007. http://www.time.com/time/magazine/article/0,9171,1601845-1,00.html

Numerous organizations are representing these issues in the courts. The Alliance Defense Fund, for example, regularly accepts cases involving the First Amendment and the 1963 *Schempp* decision to make sure that our rights are upheld within the current laws. *Legally*, there is a place for the Bible in the schools. When adhering to certain guidelines, it can be taught— but do we believe that it should be? The CBS News poll concluded:

> *Americans are more open to the idea of teaching the Bible as a piece of literature, in classes such as English or Social Studies. Sixty-four percent of Americans think public schools should be allowed to teach the Bible this way.*

Other Americans ask the question in a different way: "Why *shouldn't* the Bible be taught?" Many aspects of life in the 20th century Western world have been influenced by the Bible: laws, religion, literature, music, art, architecture, and morality. Words from the Bible show up metaphorically in our common speech. Politicians allude to them in their speeches. Stephen Prothero, Chairperson of the Boston University Department of Religion, argues that understanding the religions of the world is essential for being a well-rounded citizen:

> *In the late '70s, [students] knew nothing about religion, and it didn't matter. But then religion rushed into the public square. What purpose could it possibly serve for citizens to be ignorant of all that?*[63]

Time magazine states, "Simply put, the Bible is the most influential book ever written. Not only is the Bible the best-selling book of all time, it is the best-selling book of the year every year." It then compared the credentials of the Bible to the works of Shakespeare, which are widely taught:

---

63. *Van Biema, Time*, March 22, 2007.

- Beauty of language: Shakespeare, by a nose.

- Depth of subject matter: toss-up.

- Breadth of subject matter: the Bible.

- Numbers published, translated, etc: Bible.

- Number of people martyred for: Bible.

- Number of wars attributed to: Bible.

- Solace and hope provided to billions: Bible.

Certainly, the Bible has earned its place. *Time* added, "Shakespeare would almost surely have agreed. According to one estimate, he alludes to Scripture some 1,300 times."

Could it be that the Bible is being rejected not because of its literary credentials, but because of something else? Is there an intolerance or bias against what the Bible actually says? That's possible, but the vast majority of us like what the Bible says. According to religious literacy polls, nearly two-thirds of Americans believe the Bible holds the answers to "all or most of life's basic questions." CBS news reports that nearly half of all Americans (49%) would like to see religious and spiritual values have more influence in schools. Just 16% percent would like to see them have less influence.[64]

If we believe that the Bible *can* legally be taught in the classroom and if we also believe that it *should* be, the question then becomes "how?" Under current laws the Bible is finding its way back into the schools through at least three different types of grassroots movements.

1. Individual Students

In the past, school administrators and even some school districts have forbidden students to bring their own Bibles onto public school campuses. The courts have consistently concluded that this is a violation of students' First Amendment rights. Many

---

64. Joel Roberts, *"Split over Bibles in Schools."* CBS News.http://www.cbsnews.com/stories/2006/04/14/opinion/polls/main1500906.shtml.

students don't know that they have this right. Some who are aware still feel a strong social stigma against bringing their Scriptures to school. Nonetheless, the public school door is open to Bibles—as long as they come in the backpacks or under the arms of the students themselves.

2. Equal Access Student-led Groups

The Equal Access Act requires that secondary schools that allow "non-curricular and related clubs" to meet must also allow religious and political clubs to do so, as long as they are student-initiated and student-led. Some schools require an adult supervisor, but beyond that, the students are free to do as they wish within the boundaries of other school policies. Nationwide, students are meeting in school to read and discuss their Bibles and to pray or sing. The First Amendment Center in Arlington, Va., tracks recent court cases and has helped clarify students' rights and how they can exercise those rights according to school policies.

3. Elective Classes

Under the provision of the 1963 law, courts have ruled that it is clearly legal to study the Bible as an academic text. School districts and state governments are free to choose textbooks and fund these courses with tax dollars. Georgia was the first state to approve elective high school classes using the Bible as the primary text in 2006. In 2011, Oklahoma enacted HB 2321, a law which encourages public school districts to offer courses in Bible literacy. Tennessee, Georgia, South Carolina, and Texas have already passed similar legislation to raise public awareness.

Education organizations are developing curriculum that meets constitutional standards. The National Council on Bible Curriculum in Public Schools (NCBCPS) has created a curriculum that has been voted into 633 school districts and 2,160 public high schools in 38 states (*www.BibleInSchools.net*). Ninety three percent of school boards approached with NCBCPS's Bible curriculum have voted to implement it. Over 550,000 high school students have taken this course during school hours for credit. The course, "The Bible in History and Literature," is available in an electronic version that can be used on personal or school computers and which comes with multi-media support.

This movement is controversial. Larger school districts review curriculum and have a public review process. Much of the ongoing debate revolves around textbooks. Publishers are learning to walk the fine line between what is considered "sacred" and what is considered "secular." The courts are still involved and the publishers are learning to refine course content accordingly.

OAK TREES AND THE ACORN

THE BIBLE IN AMERICA
Featured Expert: Jerry Pattengale

Jerry Pattengale serves as the Executive Director of The National Conversations series, Executive Director of the Green Scholars Initiative, Distinguished Senior Fellow for The Institute for Studies of Religion (Baylor University), and Senior Fellow for the Sagamore Institute. He is also an Assistant Provost at Indiana Wesleyan University. He was recently named Research Associate at Tyndale House, Cambridge, and is a Research Scholar at Gordon-Conwell Theological Seminary. Jerry continues to serve as the Associate Publisher for Christian Scholar's Review *and, in 2000, received the National Student Advocate Award from The National Resource Center (USC) and Houghton Mifflin.*

Dr. Jerry Pattengale

Oftentimes we are unable to separate one item from its place or impact on other things, peoples, and events. Aristotle taught the concept that it is impossible to think of the acorn without envisioning the full oak tree; that its purpose or aim (or *telos*) defines its presence. In similar fashion, it's difficult to think of American history without considering its inextricable link to the Bible and those leaders who patterned their lives around it. From the Bible's obvious central role among the earliest settlers in this great country (especially the Puritans), the planting of churches in the pioneer communities, and the founding of great colleges such as Harvard and Princeton, to the raging debates about the Bible's presence in today's schools, it has both informed our national journey and served as an icon for every age.

We can go through nearly every U.S. presidency and pull biblical references from important speeches. The same is true of other national heroes, from war veterans and athletes to inventors and civic leaders. One cannot reasonably reflect on Martin Luther King Jr.'s "I Have a Dream" speech before the packed

Washington Mall without thinking of the Bible's influence on its riveting content, prose, and purpose. The same holds true for the founding of Habitat for Humanity, among the most successful humanitarian initiatives in our country's history, or Kids Hope, World Hope, the Salvation Army, and a litany of other programs representing institutionalized goodness.

The eminent American religious historian, Mark Noll, highlights the difficulty of trying to separate the Bible from the fabric of American history. In his address to Houston Baptist University (Aug. 16, 2007), he notes:

> *However difficult it may be to define the impact of the Bible on ordinary people precisely, Scripture has always been extraordinarily potent in American life. The printing history of the Bible, its application to politics, and its presence in popular culture all testify to that power.*

Noll reminds us that by 1800, America already had nearly 100 translations, and during the nineteenth century, the American Bible Society (founded only in 1816) distributed several million copies of the Bible. Noll's sentiments reflect the very notion of Aristotle's acorn when he concludes that same speech with these words:

> *. . . In the end the story of the Bible in America will not fully be told until some understanding exists of how the Bible has sustained the ordinary lives of ordinary people in ordinary situations.*

We are witnessing a time of serious challenges to both biblical precepts in general, and their influence in higher education in specific. In the recent book, *Debating Moral Education,* we catch a glimpse of loud challenges by noted scholars such as Stanley Fish. Within their challenge is not only a complete ban of the Bible for curricular components on ethics, history and the civility, but from having any direct influence on a student's moral choices.[65]

In 1963, our Supreme Court banned the teachers' ritual of beginning the day with quiet reflection or prayer and reading of the Bible in class for religious purposes. However, like the mighty oak trees that span the hills and valleys of our American landscape, the Bible has roots that run deep into the American soil. The Bible is one acorn that will continue to bloom in our society. With the help of those who are willing to work within the framework of the recent laws that have been enacted, it can still bloom in public schools as well.

LOOKING BACK AND AHEAD

The Bible and American education—it's impossible to separate the two. Whether the Bible is seen as the foundation (as it was in the past) or whether it is seen as a controversial issue (as it is today), the Bible's impact will always be felt; particularly if the majority of Americans who still desire to see the Bible's presence in public education have their way.

Will the Bible be restored to the place it once had in American public education, when it was not only respected for its academic value, but also revered and cherished for its message? Only time will tell.

---

65. To see Jerry Pattengale's reviews and critiques of these important works, go to www.booksandculture.com.

Five:

The BIBLE *in* SOCIETY

"The foundations of our society and government rest so much on the teachings of the Bible that it would be difficult to support them if faith in these teachings would cease to be practically universal in our country."—President Calvin Coolidge, 1923.[66]

The American Heritage Dictionary defines *society* as "a group of human beings broadly distinguished from other groups by mutual interests, participation in characteristic relationships, shared institutions, and a common culture... the institutions and culture of a distinct, self-perpetuating group."

That sounds a little bit sterile, doesn't it? Sure, it's accurate, but is that definition complete? To define American society, we must look at our heart. Who are we? What are our dreams? Where have we come from? What will things look like for our children and their children? When we look at society at this level, we discover our *values*, our *core*—the very *fiber* of who we are. When

---

66. Calvin Coolidge, 1923 statement in Charles Fadiman, e.g., *The American Treasury,* (New York: Harper and Brothers, Publishers, 1955), 127.

all things are considered, we find that our society is a tapestry of these fibers that weaves an expansive picture of who we are as a nation. And among the strongest and thickest of all the threads in that weaving, we find the Bible.

THE BIBLE IN THE BEGINNING

After Columbus brought the first Bible to American shores, the colonization of America was driven by many factors— including a steady wave of souls yearning to be free. In the 1600s, almost the entire world was ruled by kings. Asian emperors, kings of the Hawaiian Islands, monarchies of Europe—they all exhibited a top-down form of rule. Multitudes came to America from Europe to distance themselves from what they felt was heavy-handed oppression.

The common English Bible in Europe during this era was the Geneva Bible. It was a solid translation with extensive marginal notes written by religious leaders who were exiled from England during the bloody reign of Queen Mary I between 1553 and 1558. These notes make up approximately one-third of all the words in the Geneva Bible. It was a bitter and brutal time in history. Many of the notes reflected the heated differences that those in exile held with the British monarchy.

King James took the throne after Queen Mary I. He said that the notes in the Geneva Bible were "very partial, untrue, seditious, and savouring too much of dangerous and traitorous conceits." King James made ownership of the Geneva Bible a felony, and then assembled a team of scholars to make another translation without the marginal notes. Since then, the King James translation has become the most widely distributed Bible translation in the world.

Out of this European turmoil, many came to the New World of America seeking freedom through self-government. Virginia elected its first legislature in 1619. The famous "Mayflower Compact" clearly spelled out the Pilgrims' desire to be a self-

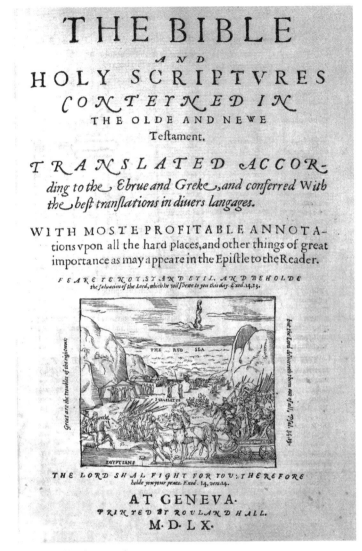

The Geneva Bible and its marginal notes

governed community. Like the Puritans and many other early immigrants, the Pilgrims looked to their Bibles for guidance and direction. They first attempted a system of shared ownership similar to the one found in the book of Acts in the New Testament:

> *All the believers were together and had everything in*
> *common. Selling their possessions and goods, they gave to*
> *anyone as he had need.*—*Acts 2:44-45*

Later, they moved to a system of private ownership, which is also modeled in other passages of the Bible. The Pilgrims' struggle to incorporate scriptural principles into government principles was just a prelude. When the call for freedom began reverberating through the Colonies, the Bible was regularly cited authoritatively. There wasn't always agreement regarding how the Bible should be interpreted or applied, but it was continually referred to as the moral standard by which other ideas and actions should be judged.

SCRIPTURE AND THE REVOLUTION

Samuel Adams is known as the "The Father of the American Revolution." As a devoted patriot, his commitment to freedom spread contagiously during the dawn of the rebellion against British rule. In a report to the Boston Town Meeting, November 20, 1772, Adams said:

> *...every man living in or out of a state of civil society has*
> *a right peaceably and quietly to worship God according to*
> *the dictates of his conscience...Just and true liberty, equal*
> *and impartial liberty, ... The Rights of the Colonists...*
> *These may be best understood by reading and carefully*
> *studying the institutes of the great Law Giver and Head*
> *of the Christian Church, which are to be found clearly*
> *written and promulgated in the New Testament.*[67]

Patrick Henry gave the American Revolution its voice. He delivered his impassioned "Give me liberty or give me death" speech just one month before the Battle of Lexington in March of 1775.

---

67. Samuel Adams, *The Rights of the Colonists. The Report of the Committee of Correspondence to the Boston Town Meeting,* Nov. 20, 1772. Old South Leaflets no. 173 (Boston: Directors of the Old South Work, 1906) 7: 418-419. http://history.hanover.edu/texts/adams.html.

We must fight! I repeat, sir, we must fight! An appeal to arms into the God of hosts is all that is left us! Besides, sir, we shall not fight our battles alone. There is a just God who presides over the destinies of nations and who will raise up friends to fight our battles for us.[68]

Patrick Henry

These were days of great upheaval and danger. The men and women who took this stand were truly putting their lives on the line as the call for liberty reached a crescendo in 1776. Those who signed the Declaration of Independence knew that if the Revolution did not succeed, they would die as traitors. On another occasion, Patrick Henry reportedly held up his Bible and said,

This book is worth all the other books which have ever been printed, and it has been my misfortune that I have

68. Patrick Henry, *Speech at the Second Virginia Convention at St. John's Church, Redmond, Virginia*, March 23, 1775.

*never found time to read it with the proper attention and
feeling till lately. I trust in the mercy of heaven that it is
not yet too late.*[69]

Noah Webster openly declared the importance of the Bible in
both religion *and* politics:

*It is extremely important to our nation, in a political
as well as religious view, that all possible authority and
influence should be given to the Scriptures; for these
furnish the best principles of civil liberty, and the most
effectual support of Republican government.*[70]

Daniel Webster has been called the "Great Defender of the
Constitution." He too pointed to the Bible as a necessary standard
of values to guide life in a free country:

*To the free and universal reading of the Bible... Men
(are) much indebted for our right view of civil liberties.
The Bible is a book which teaches man his own individual
responsibility, his dignity and his equality with his fellow
man.*[71]

John Dickinson signed the United States Constitution and
wrote the first draft of the Articles of Confederation in 1776. His
writing was a significant part of the revolutionary movement, and
some have called him "The Penman" of the Revolution. When he
argued for the private ownership of property, he appealed to the
authority of the Bible:

*... a communication of her [America's] rights in general,
and particularly of that great one, the foundation of all*

69. William Henry, *Patrick Henry: Life, Correspondence and Speeches* (New York: Charles Shatner and Sons, 1891), II: 519.
70. Noah Webster, 1832, as quoted in Verna M Hall, Principles of Liberty Drawn from the Bible, *The Christian History of the American Revolution: Consider and Ponder* (San Francisco: Foundation for American Education, 1975), 21.
71. Daniel Webster, *Address Delivered at Bunker Hill*, June 17, 1843, on the completion of the Monument (Boston: T. R. Marvin, 1843), 31.

the rest-that their property, acquired with so much pain and hazard, should be disposed of by none but themselves-or to use the beautiful and emphatic language of the sacred Scriptures, "that they should sit every man under his vine, and under his fig tree, and none should make them afraid..." (Micah 4:4) [72]

THE BIBLE AND GOVERNMENT BY THE PEOPLE

There is an old adage that says, "If you want a good argument, just bring up religion and politics." That is certainly true today, and it's been true on this continent for hundreds of years. It's safe to say that religion and politics have *always* been interwoven in the American heritage. In the pursuit of liberty and freedom, the Founding Fathers were acutely aware that a democracy had to be governed by *something*. If it wasn't ruled by a monarchy or a dominating religious presence, then what would it be? A tremendous amount of thought went into answering this question in the decades before, during, and after the Revolution, when the principles of the Bible were intentionally woven into our judicial system. John Locke wrote extensively on the topic:

[L]aws human must be made according to the general laws of Nature, and without contradiction to any positive law of Scripture, otherwise they are ill made. [73]

James Wilson signed the Declaration of Independence and the U.S. Constitution. He was an active delegate at the Constitutional Convention where he spoke 168 times. George Washington also appointed him as one of the original justices on the U.S. Supreme Court. In the textbook that he created to teach the first generation of legal students in America, James Wilson wrote:

---

72. John Dickinson, in Forrest McDonald, Ed., *Empire and Nation* (Englewood Cliffs, NJ: Prentice-Hall, 1962), 15.
73. John Locke, *Two Treatises on Government* (London: J. Whiston, etc., 1772), Book II, 285.

> *All [laws], however, may be arranged in two different*
> *classes. 1) Divine. 2) Human.... But it should always be*
> *remembered that this law, natural or revealed, made for*
> *men or for nations, flows from the same Divine source: it*
> *is the law of God. . . . Human law must rest its authority*
> *ultimately upon the authority of that law which is*
> *Divine...."*[74]

In another of his works, Wilson said:

> *In compassion to the imperfection of our internal powers,*
> *our all-gracious Creator, Preserver, and Ruler has been*
> *pleased to discover and enforce his laws, by a revelation*
> *given to us immediately and directly from himself. This*
> *revelation is contained in the holy scriptures."*[75]

Noah Webster shared the same conviction:

> *The moral principles and precepts contained in the*
> *Scriptures ought to form the basis of all our civil*
> *constitutions and laws.... All of the miseries and evils*
> *which men suffer from vice, crime, ambition, injustice,*
> *oppression, slavery, and war proceed from them despising*
> *or neglecting the precepts contained in the Bible."*[76]

Throughout the decades, this conviction held strong. Robert C. Winthrop (1809-1894) was a descendent of the first Governor of Massachusetts Bay Colony. A Harvard graduate and senator from Massachusetts, he wrote:

> *All societies of men must be governed in some way or the*
> *other. The less they may have a stringent state government,*
> *the more they must have of individual self-government.*
> *The less they rely on public law or physical force, the more*
> *they must rely on private moral restraint. Men, in a word,*

74. James Wilson, *Lectures on Law,* 1789-91.
75. James Wilson, *The Works of the Honorable James Wilson,* ed. *Bird Wilson* (Philadelphia: Lorenzo Press, 1804), Vol. I, 137-8.
76. Noah Webster, *History of the United States,* 339.

must necessarily be controlled either by a power within them, or by a power without them; either by the word of God, or by the strong arm of man; either by the Bible or the bayonet.[77]

President Calvin Coolidge

In 1927, President Calvin Coolidge said:

If American democracy is to remain the greatest hope of humanity, it must continue abundantly in the faith of the Bible.[78]

It's nearly impossible to separate the Bible from the history of our society and government; it's intertwined with just about everything. For example, when the delegates came together in Philadelphia for what is now called the "Constitutional Convention," one of the longest speeches was delivered by Benjamin Franklin. The delegates were at an impasse over almost

77. Robert C Winthrop, *Addresses and Speeches on Various Occasions, Boston,* 1852. As quoted in Verna Hall's Christian History of the American Revolution, 20.
78. Calvin Coolidge, speech in Washington, D. C., May 3, 1925, in *Treasury of Presidential Quotations,* Caroline Thomas Harnsberger, ed. (Chicago: Follett Publishing Company, 1964), 20.

every issue regarding the new Constitution. The stalemate was frustrating for all, and June 28, 1787, Franklin addressed George Washington:

> *Mr. Pres.: in this situation of the assembly groping as it were in the dark to find political truth.... In the beginning of the contest with Great Britain, we were sensible of danger, we had daily prayer in this room for the divine protection.... And have we now forgotten that powerful friend? Or do we imagine we no longer need his assistance? ....the longer I live, the more convincing proofs I see of this truth-that God governs in the affairs of men. And if a sparrow cannot fall to the ground without his notice, it is probable that an empire can rise without his aid?.... "unless the Lord build the house, they labor in vain that build it" I firmly believe this and I also believe that without his concurring aid we shall succeed in this political building no better than the builders of Babel....*

Benjamin Franklin has never been considered one of the more religious Founding Fathers. His faith and philosophies are debated to this day. Yet in this speech, he includes clear biblical references from James 1, Genesis 11, Psalm 27, and Matthew 10, as if they were just a natural part of his everyday language. And this was not an exception. Donald S. Lutz and Charles S. Hyneman, two historians from the University of Houston, did a ten-year study searching for the sources of quotes used during the founding of America. After studying 15,000 documents from the colonial era, they found 3,154 references to other sources. Of the top four, 8.3 % were from French philosopher Montesquieu, 7.9% from English jurist Sir William Blackstone, and 2.9% from English philosopher John Locke. But what source was cited more than all three of them combined? The Bible at 34%[79]—almost four times higher than the second-most quoted source.

---

79. Donald Lutz and Charles Hyneman, *American Political Writing During the Founding Era, 1760-1805.* Liberty Press, 1983.

THE DNA OF A NATION

THE BIBLE IN AMERICA
Featured Expert: Thomas S. Kidd

Thomas S. Kidd is Senior Fellow at the Institute for Studies of Religion, Baylor University, and the author of several books including Patrick Henry: First Among Patriots, *as well as* God of Liberty: A Religious History of the American Revolution. *In addition, he authored* The Great Awakening: The Roots of Evangelical Christianity in Colonial America.

Thomas S. Kidd

The Bible is so seamlessly interwoven with the American democratic tradition that one could almost miss it. Consider Patrick Henry's "Give Me Liberty or Give Me Death" speech, which was delivered in 1775 to call on Virginians to take up defensive measures against the fearsome British military. It wasn't that long of a speech—about four pages in print—but it is full of references to the Bible.

Henry didn't cite chapters and verses in the speech. Members of the Virginia Convention didn't need that. They knew the Bible when they heard it. Phrases from the Bible just flowed naturally from the mouth of this patriot, who could not separate his understanding of freedom from the principles of Scripture.

British promises of good will, he cautioned, would "prove a snare to your feet" (Jeremiah 18:22). Had Americans become like those who, he asked, "having eyes, see not, and having ears, hear not" (Jeremiah 5:21)? And he warned that "gentlemen may cry, peace, peace—but there is no peace" (Jeremiah 6:14). Even the speech's final line had a hint of Joshua 24:15 in it: "I know not what course others may take; but as for me, give me liberty, or give me death!"

Henry's use of the Bible reflects a broader historical trajectory. Many of the texts and speeches that undergird American democracy resonate with the rhetoric of Scripture. Massachusetts' first governor, John Winthrop, told his fellow settlers that "we shall be as a city upon a hill; the eyes of all people are upon us" (Matthew 5:14). The "Great Communicator," Ronald Reagan, repeatedly reminded Americans of Winthrop's story and this Bible passage, and it became one of his most famous quotes, too.

Sometimes even skeptics, or those who struggled to believe in traditional Christianity, have used the Bible in great speeches and texts because they understood the compelling power of Scripture among the American people. Tom Paine, for example, became a notorious religious skeptic in America in the 1790s, but in 1776 he borrowed liberally from the Bible to make his argument for independence in *Common Sense*, the most influential political pamphlet in American history. In one of the tract's most stirring passages, Paine addressed those who wondered how America would fare without a king. He proposed that as Americans removed George III's crown, they should place the crown instead on "the divine law, the word of God... by which the world may

know, that so far we approve of monarchy, that in America
THE LAW IS KING."

Similarly, even though Abraham Lincoln never joined a church
due to personal scruples, he mastered the use of the Bible in his
speeches, especially in his haunting Second Inaugural Address.
This 1865 speech, delivered a month before the end of the Civil
War and a month before Lincoln's own death, explained the war's
massive sacrifices and loss of life by reference to the Bible. Indeed,
he noted the irony that both sides in the war "read the same Bible,
and pray to the same God." Like most Americans, he hoped the
war would end soon. "Yet, if God wills that it continue, until all
the wealth piled by the bond-man's two hundred and fifty years of
unrequited toil shall be sunk, and until every drop of blood drawn
with the last, shall be paid by another drawn with the sword, as
was said three thousand years ago, so still it must be said 'the
judgments of the Lord, are true and righteous altogether'" (Psalm
19:9).

Even today, as Americans work to accommodate the realities
of religious diversity and non-belief, the Bible offers comfort and
meaning in times of national tragedy. We saw this on the tenth
anniversary of the 9/11 terrorist attacks, when President Barack
Obama read Psalm 46, which opens with the assurance that "God
is our refuge and strength, a very present help in trouble."

The Bible does not provide answers to all political questions,
but at a more fundamental level, it has helped define our nation's
guiding principles, given moral direction to our freedom, and
offered peace in times of grief. Thusly, the Bible is, indeed,
foundational to the American democratic tradition.

America's Founding Fathers not only believed that the Bible
was foundational to American society, but they also believed that

society should be built upon it for generations to come. Elias
Boudinot was the fourth President of the Continental Congress,
a signer of the peace treaty to end the American Revolution, the
first attorney admitted to the U.S. Supreme Court Bar, a framer
of the Bill of Rights, and the Director of the U.S. Mint. What was
his personal view of the Scriptures?

> *For nearly half a century have I anxiously and critically
> studied that invaluable treasure [the Bible]; and I still
> scarcely ever take it up that I do not find something new –
> that I do not receive some valuable addition to my stock of
> knowledge or perceive some instructive fact never observed
> before. In short, were you to ask me to recommend the most
> valuable book in the world, I should fix on the Bible as
> the most instructive both to the wise and ignorant. Were
> you to ask me for one affording the most rational and
> pleasing entertainment to the inquiring mind, I should
> repeat, it is the Bible; and should you renew the inquiry
> for the best philosophy or the most interesting history,
> I should still urge you to look into your Bible. I would
> make it, in short, the Alpha and Omega of knowledge.[80]*

Many Founding Fathers dedicated their time and efforts to
encourage Bible reading and distribution. James McHenry (1753-
1816), for example, was an officer in the Revolutionary War. He
signed the Constitution and was Secretary of War under George
Washington and James Adams. He said:

> *Public utility pleads most forcibly for the general
> distribution of the Holy Scriptures. The doctrine they
> preach, the obligations they impose, the punishment they
> threaten, the rewards they promise, the stamp and image
> of divinity they bear, which produces a conviction of their*

---

80. Bernard C. Steiner, *One Hundred and Ten Years of Bible Society Work in Maryland, 1810-
1920* (Maryland Bible Society, 1921), 14.

truths, can alone secure to society, order and peace, and to our courts of justice and constitutions of government, purity, stability and usefulness. In vain, without the Bible, we increase penal laws and draw entrenchments around our institutions. Bibles are strong entrenchments. Where they abound, men cannot pursue wicked courses, and at the same time enjoy quiet conscience.

McHenry was also the first President of the Bible Society in Baltimore and made it his goal to facilitate the spread of the Bible to all Americans:

Consider also, the rich do not possess ought more precious than their Bible, and that the poor cannot be presented by the rich with anything of greater value. Withhold it not from the poor. It is a book of councils and directions, fitted to every situation in which men can be placed. It is an Oracle which reveals to mortals the secrets of heaven and the hidden will of the Almighty.... It is for the purpose of distributing this divine book more effectually and extensively among the multitudes, whose circumstances render such a donation necessary, that your cooperation is most earnestly requested.[81]

The work of the Bible societies has been remarkably successful and continues today across the country and the globe. Ethnicity divides us. Politics divide us. Economics divide us. But with a Bible in nearly every home, it is, perhaps, the one document that unifies us. Even during the Civil War, the Bible was a unifying influence; something shared by the masses in spite of violent, bloody disagreement. General Robert E. Lee reportedly confessed, "In all my perplexities and distresses, the Bible has never failed to give me light and strength." North of the battle lines, Ulysses S. Grant exhorted, "Hold fast to the Bible. . . . To the influence

---

81. James McHenry in Bernard Steiner, *One Hundred and Ten Years of Bible Society Work in Maryland, 1810-1920* (Maryland Bible Society, 1921), 14.

of this Book we are indebted for all the progress made in true civilization and to this we must look as our guide in the future." In his second inaugural address, as brother fought brother in the bloodiest conflict ever on American soil, Abraham Lincoln reflected on the common ground that connected the hearts of all Americans:

> *Both read the same Bible and pray to the same God, and each invokes His aid against the other. It may seem strange that any men should dare to ask a just God's assistance in wringing their bread from the sweat of other men's faces, but let us judge not, that we be not judged. The prayers of both could not be answered. ... Fondly do we hope, fervently do we pray, that this mighty scourge of war may speedily pass away.*

Like so many of the statesman who came before him, Lincoln's words were saturated with biblical references, both direct and indirect, as he communicated his heart during those perilous years.

THE BATTLE FOR THE BIBLE

Less than a century after Lincoln, the natural infusion of the Bible in American politics and government would be seriously challenged. The First Amendment to the Constitution says, "Congress shall make no law respecting the establishment of religion or prohibiting the free exercise thereof." For 150 years, this amendment was interpreted literally, because there were virtually no Supreme Court cases regarding the religion clause prior to the 1940s. It was understood as a protection to keep the government from interfering with people's personal religious beliefs and to prohibit a government-sanctioned religion (like many of those in Europe). The interpretation and application of the First Amendment began to shift as early as 1947, through the

Supreme Court case of *Everson v. Board of Education*. The Court's decision in this case not only maintained that the government needed to stay out of peoples' religion. The Court's comments also pointed toward an even stronger separation to come:

> *The First Amendment has erected a wall between church and state. That wall must be kept high and impregnable. We could not approve the slightest breach.*

Since the *Everson* decision, First Amendment cases have flooded the courts. Chief Justice Earl Warren (1891-1974) stepped into this beehive of controversy during the upheaval of the 1950s and 1960s. He headed the commission that investigated the assassination of John F. Kennedy. His court ended racial segregation in public schools and transformed important areas of American law, such as those regarding the rights of the accused. In dealing with First Amendment issues, the Warren Court outlawed mandatory school prayer in *Engel v. Vitale* in 1962—a decision that is still passionately debated today.

Although Warren's interpretation of the Constitution is still controversial, his beliefs about the Bible were clear. In 1954, *Time* printed a speech that Warren gave to a gathering of 600 people— including the President, the Vice President, the Chief Justice of the Supreme Court, Congressmen, foreign diplomats, and noted businessmen. Warren said:

> *I believe no one can read the history of our country without realizing that the Good Book and the spirit of the Savior have from the beginning been our guiding geniuses.... I believe the entire Bill of Rights came into being because of the knowledge our forefathers had of the Bible and their belief in it; freedom of belief, of expression, of assembly, of petition, the dignity of the individual, the sanctity of the home, equal justice under law, and the reservation of powers to the people....*

I like to believe we are living today in the spirit of the Christian religion. I like also to believe that as long as we do so, no great harm can come to our country.[82]

Chief Justice Earl Warren

Warren saw that the Bible was embedded in American society as clearly as the Leviticus passage that had been cast into the Liberty Bell: "Proclaim liberty throughout the land and to all the inhabitants thereof." Woodrow Wilson, 28th President and President of Princeton University, held similar beliefs:

> *The Bible… is one of the supreme sources of revelation of the meaning of life, the nature of God, and the spiritual nature and needs of men. It is the only guide of life which really leads the spirit in the way of peace and salvation.*[83]

82. *Religion: Breakfast in Washington.* Time, February 15, 1954, available at http://www.time.com/time/magazine/article/0,9171,936197,00.html.
83. Woodrow Wilson, remarks at a Denver rally, 1911 in *The Supreme Court and Public Prayer,* Charles E. Rice (New York: Fordham University Press, 1964), 61-62.

Wilson boldly proclaimed this in a public rally over 100 years ago. But do we, as Americans in the 21st century, still believe that today? In our survey with America's Research Group, 1,000 Americans gave us the answer.

Do you believe the Bible still applies to today's problems or is it something that was practical years ago?

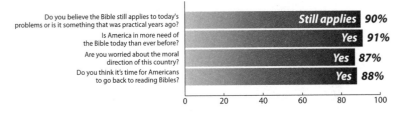

Study after study reveals that Americans still believe that the Bible has a role in the modern world, and that we need its influence as a country more than ever. An interesting study done by the Barna group for ABS showed that over half of Americans (54%) believe that the Bible has too little influence in our society today, which is four times the number who believe it has too much influence (13%). Those who believe the Bible's influence is just about right were 28%.[84]

By and large, our beliefs as a nation echo those of Theodore Roosevelt, the 26th U. S. President:

> *If we read the Bible aright, we read a book which teaches us to go forth and do the work of the Lord, to do the work of the Lord in the world as we find it; to try to make things better in this world, even if only a little better because we have lived in it…we plead for a closer and wider and deeper study of the Bible, so that our people may be in fact as well as in theory, doers of the Word and not hearers only.[85]*

---

84. American Bible Society, The Barna Group, *The State of the Bible 2011* (New York, NY, 2011), 7.
85. Frank Glenn Lankard, *Bible and Life and Ideals of English-speaking People* (New York: American Bible Society, 1948), 7.

A vocal minority in America seems to capture the headlines, proclaiming that the Bible has become irrelevant, undesirable, and inappropriate in the public arena of American society. But the statistics simply don't support that. Neither do the words of our leaders. In a speech given February 2, 2012, President Obama quoted the Bible at least eight times:

> *...I believe in God's command to "love thy neighbor as thyself."...And when I talk about shared responsibility... it also coincides with Jesus's teaching that "for unto whom much is given, much shall be required." ... But part of that belief comes from my faith in the idea that I am my brother's keeper and I am my sister's keeper... It's also about the biblical call to care for the least of these – for the poor; for those at the margins of our society. To answer the responsibility we're given in Proverbs to "Speak up for those who cannot speak for themselves, for the rights of all who are destitute."... The Bible teaches us to "be doers of the word and not merely hearers." We're required to have a living, breathing, active faith in our own lives. And each of us is called on to give something of ourselves for the betterment of others—and to live the truth of our faith not just with words, but with deeds. John tells us that, "If anyone has material possessions and sees his brother in need but has no pity on him, how can the love of God be in him? Dear children, let us not love with words or tongue but with actions and in truth."*

John Quincy Adams

LOOKING TO THE FUTURE

The biblical legacy each of us has inherited from our forefathers is powerfully reflected upon in the letters of John Quincy Adams. John Quincy was the son of John Adams, a leading champion for independence and the second President of the United States. As a child, he watched carefully as the Revolution emerged, the war was won, and the United States came into being. He became our sixth President, and when he became a father himself, he wrote extensive letters to his own son, George Washington Adams, intentionally passing on the legacy to the next generation. While serving as a diplomat in Saint Petersburg, Russia, September 1811, John Quincy wrote:

My Dear Son:

In your letter of the 18th January to your mother, you mentioned that you read to your aunt a chapter in the Bible or a section of Doddridge's Annotations every evening. This information gave me real pleasure; for so great is my veneration for the Bible, and so strong my belief, that when duly read and meditated on, it is of all books in the world, that which contributes most to make men good, wise, and happy - that earlier my children begin to read it, the more steadily they pursue the practice of reading it throughout their lives, the more lively and confident will be my hopes that they will prove useful citizens to their country, respectable members of society, and a real blessing to their parents.... I have always endeavored to read it with the same spirit and temper of mind, which I now recommend to you: that is, with the intention and desire that it may contribute to my advancement in wisdom and virtue.... I can only pray Almighty God, for the aid of his Spirit to strengthen my good desires, and to subdue my propensities to evil; for it is from him, that every good and every perfect gift descends. My custom is, to read four or five chapters every morning, immediately after rising from my bed. It employs about an hour of my time, and seems to me the most suitable manner of beginning the day.... You have already come to that age in many respects; you know that difference between right and wrong, and you know some of your duties, and the obligation you are under, to become acquainted with them all. It is in the Bible you must learn them and from the Bible how to practice them. Those duties are to God, to your fellow creatures, and to yourself.

Let us, then, search the Scriptures.... The Bible contains the revelation of the will of God. It contains the history of the creation of the world, and of mankind... It contains a system of religion, and of morality, which we may examine upon its own merits.... it contains a numerous collection of books, written at different ages of the world, by different authors, which we may survey as curious monuments of antiquity, and as literary compositions. In what light so ever we regard it, whether with reference to revelation, to literature, to history, or to morality - it is an invaluable and inexhaustible mine of knowledge and virtue.

From your affectionate Father,
John Quincy Adams.[86]

From Plymouth Rock in 1620 to 1600 Pennsylvania Avenue today, the Bible's influence is woven through the fiber of our democracy and our society. Every time a new president places his hands on a Bible, swearing to uphold the duties of his office, another thread of that biblical legacy is stitched into the tapestry of American democracy. Each time a soldier says a prayer and tucks a Bible into his vest pocket, the tapestry of the Bible in America grows a little larger. And every time a parent opens a Bible with a child and talks about its timeless principles and passes on its epic history, the future history of our society is influenced. Who determines the role the Bible will hold in America? We all do. The future of the Bible in our society clearly rests in all of our hands.

86. John Quincy Adams. *Letters of John Quincy Adams to His Son, On the Bible and Its Teachings* (Auburn, NY: Derby, Miller, & Co. 1848), 11. 20-21.

Six:

The BIBLE *and* YOU

"It's extremely bold to predict, but we believe the potential is there to be the most Bible engaged generation in history." – Bobby Gruenewald, Creator of YouVersion, *the world's fastest growing Bible application*

The Bible has had an unquestionable influence on our science, education, democracy, arts, and society. As a nation, the legacy of the Bible saturates us like water in a sponge. Its impact on our society as a whole is evident from the time of Columbus to today. But America is more than a "society." We aspire to live in a country where the rights of the individual matter, and the values and actions of a single person are respected. We have always been (and always will be) more than a nation of faceless masses defined by political and physical borders. We strive to be an intertwined community of *individuals*—individuals who have been granted the right to life, liberty, and the pursuit of happiness. With those rights come responsibilities for the things that have been entrusted to us. Yes, the benefits we enjoy from living in American society are many—yet there are certain things that we can and must do for ourselves.

Engaging the Bible on a personal level is one of those things. No one can experience it for us.

SCRIPTURE ENGAGEMENT

We have been given the right to read the Scripture. We have the freedom to contemplate it, digest it, and apply it. That's an opportunity that many people do not have. In some countries, these thoughts and actions often cost people their lives.

Our survey with ARG shows that Americans think we should take advantage of this opportunity. When asked the question, "Do you think it's time for Americans to go back to reading Bibles?" 88% of us said "Yes." It's as if we intuitively understand that there is a connection between the roots of the Bible in our past and our desires to live meaningful, joyful lives that celebrate freedom today. Numerous surveys have shown a direct correlation between reading the Bible and many of the things that we value as a country.

In 2002, *The National Religion Survey* by Edison Media Research found that 60% of Americans believe the Bible is "very important" in decision making. Another 23% said it is "somewhat" important.[87] In addition, the Barna Group found that people who read the Bible regularly were more than twice as likely to experience a faith-based "transformation" as those who do not.[88] One survey even found that reading the Bible can be linked to a decrease in debt.[89]

These types of correlations surface in survey after survey. Reading the Bible is closely associated with the things we value the most in life. To be fair, most of these studies can only show

---

87. Edison Media Research, *The National Religion Survey* (2002), 20.
88. The Barna Group, *Half of Americans Say Faith Has "Greatly Transformed" Their Life* (Ventura, CA, 2006), 1.
89. Kluth, Brian. *Bible Reading Helps Your Financial Health*. State of the Plate, www.stateoftheplate.info (2010).

correlation, not a cause/effect relationship. Simple surveys are not designed to prove that personal Bible reading causes happiness, better marriages and less debt, but they do indicate that Bible reading goes hand-in-hand with them. When we repetitively see Bible usage linked with these positive real-life elements, it's not difficult to make the connection.

Furthermore, the statistics show that our desire to read the Bible appears to be motivated by something much deeper. In 2011, the Barna Group conducted a survey for American Bible Society's State of the Bible report. One section of the survey investigated various motivations for reading the Scriptures, and the results revealed a hunger for something much more than just the American dream:

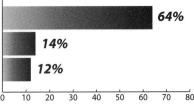

Read the Bible because it brings them closer to God — **64%**
Read the Bible because they need comfort — **14%**
Read the Bible to get direction or solve a problem.[90] — **12%**

Our contention that the Bible brings us "closer to God" should not be a surprise. It is rooted in our experience. This belief is grounded in what we believe to be true about the Bible itself. Surveys by the Gallup Organization clearly reveal that we believe the Bible is more than a book. Furthermore, we feel that there is more to its stories than mere historical recordings of events. We hold its prophecies as more than just predictions. We consider the wisdom in its words to be more than just good advice. According to Gallup:

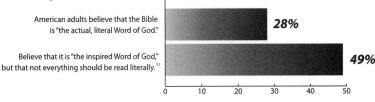

American adults believe that the Bible is "the actual, literal Word of God." — **28%**
Believe that it is "the inspired Word of God," but that not everything should be read literally.[91] — **49%**

90. American Bible Society, The Barna Group, *The State of the Bible 2011* (New York, NY, 2011) 18.
91. The Gallup Organization, *28% Believe Bible Is Actual Word of God.* (2006) 1-3.

When you add those numbers together, we get to the core of why adults hunger for this book far more than any other: 77% of adults believe the Bible is God's message to us in written form. Half of all Americans believe the Bible is "inspired" by God, but that not *everything* should be taken "literally." (This is partially due to the fact that the Bible contains a good amount of symbolic and figurative language, such as the passages that say "God is our rock" or that we can find shelter "under His wings.")

But what about our current teenagers? Is our biblical heritage and belief in the Bible being lost? What do the future leaders of our country believe about the Bible?

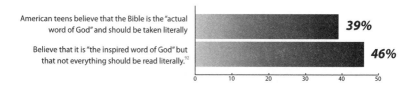

Add those two numbers together and we find that a full 85% of American teens believe that the Bible contains the words of God. Young and old, we feel that this book is the *authentic* message from God to us. An increasing portion of us also consider it to be an *accurate* message from God. According to the Barna Group, in 2007, 18% of adults said that the Bible contained factual or historic errors. Only 14% believed that in 2011. In 2007, 11% stated that the Bible is *not* inspired by God. That number dropped to 8% in 2011.

These are very significant numbers. When 77% of adults and 85% of teenagers believe the Bible is the word of God, it only makes sense that we want to read it to get closer to God, to experience God's comfort, and to receive God's guidance. When Baylor University and Gallup[93] asked about this, the results were remarkable.

---

92. Winseman, Albert, *Teens Stance on the Word of God*, The Gallup Organization (2005).
93. Wuthnow, *Robert, Arts and Religion Survey 1999*, The Gallup Organization (Princeton, NJ, 1999).

"How important has reading the Bible on your own been to growing spiritually and to developing a closer relationship with God?

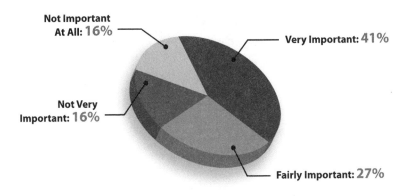

Not Important At All: 16%

Very Important: 41%

Not Very Important: 16%

Fairly Important: 27%

While historians and archeologists may study the Bible for academic reasons, it is the belief that the Bible contains a divine message that motivates most people to read it themselves.

A BIG BUMPY BIBLE

Helen Keller is one of America's most beloved and unique personalities and was chosen by *Time* magazine as one of the most influential people of the twentieth century. Unable to see or hear, her life was a black, silent void until her faithful tutor finally helped her connect with the outside world through touch. She went on to live a life of legendary optimism. She deeply appreciated having a Bible she could "read." It was over six feet tall and was printed in the raised letters of Braille. Her poignant letter of gratitude was printed in the *New York Times* (February 9, 1902). She once wrote:

Unless we form the habit of going to the Bible in bright moments as well as in trouble, we cannot fully respond to its consolations because we lack equilibrium between light and darkness.

Helen Keller

Sixty eight percent of us *feel* like the Bible is very or fairly important in getting closer to God. But is that a *fact?* Does the Bible actually *cause* spiritual growth? Starting in 2004, the Willow Creek Association began using the *REVEAL Spiritual Life Survey* to gather data from over a quarter of a million people who attended over 1,000 different congregations from all denominations.[94] They identified three different shifts that take place between four phases in spiritual growth:

1. People begin by *exploring* spiritual things.

2. They then shift to *growing* in a personal relationship with God.

3. Next, they become *close* to God.

4. Finally, they shift to being *centered* on God.

---

94. The implications of this study are discussed in the book Move, *What 1000 Churches Reveal about Spiritual Growth*, by Hawkins and Parkinson. Zondervan, 2011. www.willowcreek.com.

What causes these shifts to take place? Several different factors seemed to make a difference, but one in particular emerged as the primary catalyst for spiritual growth. Cally Parkinson, who headed the research team with Greg L. Hawkins, explains how engaging the Bible, in a personal way has more impact on spiritual growth than any other practice:

> *Everywhere we turned, the data revealed the same results: Spending time in the Bible is hands-down the highest impact personal spiritual practice. More specifically, 'I reflect on the meaning of Scripture in my life' is the spiritual practice that is most predictive of growth for all three spiritual movements.... There's great significance in the word* reflection. *Reflecting on Scripture implies a contemplative process, one of thoughtful and careful deliberation.... This is not about skimming through a Bible passage or devotional in a mechanical way. This is a powerful experience of personal meditation that catalyzes spiritual growth, starting at the very beginning of the spiritual journey.... Nothing matters more to their spiritual development —including church services, serving activities, small groups—than spending time in God's word. Nothing beats the Bible.*[95]

The Arts and Religion Survey of 1999[96] by Gallup and Robert Wuthnow showed that 39% of Americans are taking advantage of this "meditation that catalyzes for spiritual growth" by reading the Bible while praying or meditating. How often do we seize the opportunity to read God's words for ourselves? Our survey conducted by ARG found these cumulative percentages:

95. Greg L. Hawkins and Cally Parkinson, *Follow Me* (Willow Creek Resources, 2008), 117.
96. Wuthnow, Robert, *Arts and Religion Survey* 1999.

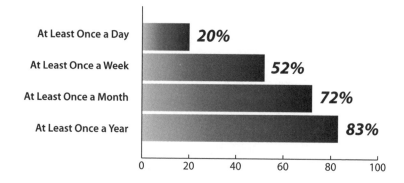

According to these numbers, only 17% read the Bible less than once a year. The Arts and Religion Survey of 1999 came back with numbers that were considerably lower, but they asked the question differently:

How often do you read the Bible in your daily life when you are at home?

	Percent	Cumulative Percent
Every Day	14%	14%
Nearly Every Day	9%	23%
About Once A Week	12%	35%
Several Times A Month	8%	43%
About Once A Month	6%	49%
Several Times A Year	11%	60%
Hardly Ever or Never	40%	100%

A study by the Barna Group in 2007[97] revealed similar results as did our study in 2010. A 2011 study showed that 25% of Americans never read the Bible on their own and only 41% of Americans read the Bible outside of church.[98]

This is where we start to see a disheartening rift in the data. A discrepancy emerges between what we say we believe about the Bible and our actions. For example, Gallup found that two-thirds of Americans agree that the Bible "answers all or most of the basic questions of life," yet 28% who agreed with the statement said they rarely or never read the Bible.[99] Many Americans report they would like to learn more about the Bible, with 35% saying they are "very interested" in deepening their understanding of the Bible. Forty percent say they are "somewhat interested" (only 24% have no interest in learning more about the Bible). Sadly, our reading habits do not reflect our desire to make spiritual strides by actively engaging in the Bible.

Not only do we have a deep desire for our own personal growth, but we would like to see spiritual growth in our families as well. The ARG survey asked, "Which one of these areas would you like your children to learn more?" The response was as follows:

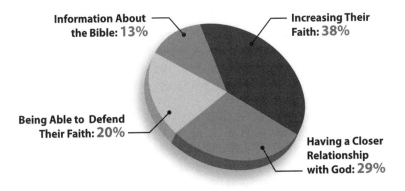

Information About the Bible: 13%

Increasing Their Faith: 38%

Being Able to Defend Their Faith: 20%

Having a Closer Relationship with God: 29%

97. American Bible Society, The Barna Group, *Barna's Annual Tracking Study Shows Americans Stay Spiritually Active, but Biblical Views Wane* (Ventura, CA, 2007).
98. American Bible Society, The Barna Group, *The State of the Bible 2011*, 15.
99. Wuthnow, Robert, *Arts and Religion Survey* 1999.

Every survey we can find shows that the vast majority of American parents want to see their children grow spiritually. Is this desire reflected in our actions? The ARG 2010 study asked parents who have children at home, "How often do you read the Bible to your children?" The percentages were:

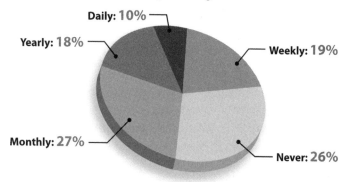

Twenty-six percent never read the Bible to their children. Clearly, some parents are taking an active role in helping their children develop spiritually through the Bible. But many are not. During the Middle Ages, the common person didn't have access to the Bible. Now we have it, but we don't engage it nearly as much as we could, and not nearly as much as we would like. We are now at a crucial point as individuals and as a nation. Are we headed back toward the New Middle Ages or toward the New Enlightenment?

Actually, it appears that Americans are facing some very real challenges in the pursuit to study the Word more deeply.

BARRIERS TO SCRIPTURE ENGAGEMENT

When Barna was surveying for The State of the Bible 2011 report[100], they listed a number of frustrations people have with the Bible and asked respondents to prioritize them:

---

100. American Bible Society, The Barna Group, *The State of the Bible 2011*, 19.

- 37% said they never seem to have enough time to read it. This single frustration surpassed all others. By comparing these results to a similar Barna study in 1999, we can see that the busyness factor is increasing.

- 13% had difficulty relating to the language.

- 9% weren't excited about it.

- 9% didn't understand the historical background.

- 8% couldn't find the stories they were looking for.

- Nearly 1/5 of adults (19%) said they have no frustrations in reading the Bible.

Part of the problem with "understanding the language" is likely because 57% of Americans own The King James Version, the most popular English translation of the Bible in the world.[101] The King James translation was finished in 1611. The English language has changed a lot since then, so many of the words in the KJV feel strange and awkward to modern readers.

Modern translations solve this problem. "Word-for-word" translations, such as *The New King James Version, The New American Standard, The Amplified Bible* and *The New American Bible* retain much of the word order from the Hebrew and Greek. They are preferred by scholars and students. "Phrase-by-phrase" translations like *The New International Version, The Contemporary English Version* and *The New Living Translation* structure sentences in a way that is more natural for English speakers. "Paraphrase" Bibles, like *The Living Bible* and *The Message*, are translated "idea-by-idea" and read smoothly and naturally. The trade-off is that they are less accurate. Specific translations can be sampled at sites like *www.youversion.com* and *www.biblegateway.com*.

---

101. American Bible Society, The Barna Group, *The State of the Bible 2011*, 13.

GOING DIGITAL

The information age has flooded us with too many things to read and not enough time to read them. It's no wonder that "lack of time" is the number one thing holding us back from reading the Bible as much as we want to. Thankfully, the same technology that overwhelms us now makes it extremely easy and convenient to engage the Bible. Technology and resources are moving so quickly that the progress is almost dizzying. The things which astound us today will become commonplace tomorrow as the Bible goes virtual and viral. Verses can be texted to us automatically throughout the day. "E-devotions" add thoughtful commentary to passages and suggest prayers to add a personal appeal. Applications and programs for smart phones, tablets and computers allow us to engage scripture in ways no one would have dreamed of a few decades ago. Here are a few current examples:

BIBLE APPLICATIONS: www.YouVersion.com

YouVersion is the number one Bible application today. Tens of millions of people are using it to make the Bible part of their daily lives.

- It's free, easy to use, and works on nearly every phone or computer.

- It supports hundreds of different Bible translations in many different languages.

- It has hundreds of different reading plans.

- It can automatically send Bible verses for daily reading.

- It is convenient for sharing verses on Twitter and Facebook.

- It is possible to highlight, label and make notes in the text.

SOCIAL MEDIA: www.facebook.com/TheBible

"The Bible" Facebook page is currently the most visited page in the Facebook universe, beating out every pop star and politician. It's a virtual world unto itself where millions share their spiritual journey in the Bible.

ONLINE BIBLES: www.BibleGateway.com
www.BlueLetterBible.com

A quick search of the internet reveals a massive number of websites dedicated to the Bible. Many of them come with access to search engines that allow searchers to find topics, commentaries, and links to the original languages of Hebrew and Greek.

DIGITAL BIBLES: www.GloBible.com

The GloBible is a highly interactive digital Bible supported by large amounts of multimedia content. It uses "lenses" which organize data in a way that allows for intuitive searches or random exploration of the world of the Bible on multiple levels.

- The "Bible Lens" presents the content of the Bible in four different translations, in a way that allows you to get to any chapter of the Bible in two clicks. Links from each verse take you directly to the media resources related to that passage.

- The "Atlas Lens" distributes the content of the Bible geographically. You can see where the major stories of the Bible happened and navigate through them with virtual tours, photos, and expert video on key sites.

- The "Timeline Lens" organized the content of the Bible chronologically, so you can see when events happened in context with one another through a "zoomable" interface.

- The "Media Lens" accesses a vast collection of videos, virtual realities, and photos.
- The "Topic Lens" organizes the content by person, place or thing, distributing content in a network that navigates smoothly and quickly.

These five lenses can also be utilized to filter content. For example, if a person wondered what Jesus had to say on the subject of redemption during the Passion Week in Jerusalem, the answer is readily available. What would be an otherwise impossible search can be done quickly, visually, and intuitively. There is even an option to create a customized reading plan based on the user's searches. The GloBible is also available in a free "lite" version for all common cell phone, tablet, and computer platforms.

These are unprecedented days for the Bible. It exists in more translations, more formats, with more resources and references than ever before, and the options just keep growing. In many ways, the challenge of reading the Bible today is quite the opposite of the past, when getting access to Scripture was difficult and expensive.

GETTING INTO THE BIBLE

THE BIBLE IN AMERICA
Featured Expert: Lamar Vest

Lamar Vest has been a long-term leader in developing and expanding Bible missions in the United States and around the world. He is a past president and CEO of the American Bible Society. Some of Lamar Vest's other services include acting as chairman of the National Association of Evangelicals and holding an executive leadership position for the Church of God (Cleveland, Tenn.). He has also served as acting President of Lee University.

Dr. Lamar Vest

AMERICAN BIBLE SOCIETY

Nearly 200 years ago, the American Bible Society (ABS) began its mission. Deep in our organization's DNA is an unbreakable charter to make sure that the bold, holy experiment called "the United States of America" never loses a fundamental and critical taproot in God's Word. ABS and I have perfect confidence that the big, sweeping narrative of the Bible is "dialed-in" to our highest hopes and aspirations. All that we long to see in our world—love, forgiveness, compassion and humility—can be found in the Bible.

I often remind the American Bible Society staff of my fear of accepting the status quo. Without a general climate of urgency, the danger is that we may do nothing until it is too late. It is said that the people of Pompeii made a reasonable, but tragic estimate of the risk that Vesuvius *might* erupt. Their failure to comprehend a very real danger and to take evasive action proved to be catastrophic. America is in a similar situation. Times are changing and so ABS's mission is expanding. ABS will always translate, publish and distribute Bibles, but since almost every person either owns a Bible or can access it online, we are now faced with some new questions: Is the Bible having the impact on individuals and society as it once did? How do we help people engage it on a meaningful level?

Our research continues to reveal that people are not coming to a clear understanding of God because they have lost the big picture—the meta-narrative—the grand story that ties it all together. The Bible tells us how we got here and why, what we're supposed to do and where we are going. To lose touch with this story is indeed to lose touch with the concept of hope all together. The first thing that we have to do is let people know the Bible is not just a dusty old rulebook. It's not something given for our punishment. No one should grit their teeth and say, "I'm going to get through this chapter today if it kills me!" The Word of God is alive! It's the story of God, and once we get the big picture, it shows how to actually become part of the grand story. More than actively reading it, we want to allow Scripture to engage us—to breathe life into us!

This is precisely why we are inviting thousands of leaders from across the nation to join with us in a movement to "Uncover the Word." This is an invitation to see the best of the Bible come alive in our hearts, homes and communities. This movement includes a wide range of partners and resources, all featured at *www. UncoverTheWord.org*. Driving this movement are the questions: If we're successful in waking the sleeping giant of Scripture engagement, what could America look like? What if our actions did a better job of reflecting what most of us acknowledge as God's Word?

If we truly became engrossed in the Bible, would we resolve conflict more peacefully by turning the other cheek? Would we love our neighbor as ourselves—even if it meant checking our frustration when the driver in front of us slows down our commute? Would we take the time to offer a kind word or to ask about a sick neighbor? Would we clear a spot in our hectic schedules to keep an eye on an elderly widow? Where would visiting a prisoner fall on our list of priorities?

The media seems to emphasize complaints about a prayer offered at a graduation, the mention of God by a public official, or the presence of a cross in a military memorial. We're often left with the impression that many Americans want religion to stay out of everyday life. Statistics show otherwise—and I've yet to meet someone concerned about too little encouragement, too little hope and too little confidence in the greatness of God's love. The big, sweeping narrative of the Bible is, in fact, "dialed-in" to our highest hopes and aspirations.

So how do we achieve a better alignment between our beliefs and observable actions? A good start is to move from being a Bible owner to a Bible reader! The presence of a dusty Bible on the shelf won't make a person live more biblically any more than the presence of a diet book in the home will make one live more healthily. For the Bible to get into our hearts and lives, we need to get into the Bible and let the Bible get into us.

A PLACE TO START TODAY: WWW.UNCOVERTHEWORD.COM

When the American Bible Society was founded 200 years ago, their mission was simple: They wanted to get a Bible in the hands of every American. That mission is nearly complete. Now that people have Bibles *available*, they want to help people *encounter* the Bible on a regular basis. Dozens of organizations are coming together to pursue this new vision. They are developing helpful resources to help *engage* the Bible on a personal level.

Strategies range from the academic "Inductive Bible Study Method" to the meditative "*Lecto Divina*" (Latin for "sacred reading"), an ancient form of praying and contemplating Scripture practiced by Catholic monks in the third century. It begins by carefully and slowly reading a passage of the Bible such as the prayers of David in Psalm 51, the wisdom of Solomon in Proverbs 3, the teaching of Jesus in Matthew 6, or the encouragement of Paul in Philippians 3. This is followed by thoughtful meditation about the meaning of the passage, then by prayer, contemplation, and then action. It is a powerful practice that is seeing a resurgence of interest today among people of all ages and backgrounds.

Scripture engagement really comes down to this: In America, we have been given the right to read the Bible if we choose. We have been given the freedom to contemplate it, digest it, and apply it if we wish. These are simple things that any individual can do—but no one else can do them for us.

ISN'T IT TIME?

These are critical days for our nation—and for each and every one of us who call America our home. In the past, the Bible was there to guide us. As our all-time bestseller (and the most widely read book on the continent), the Bible is the most important book in the history of America. It influenced our science, formed the core of our education system, shaped our democracy, and permeated our society. While the Bible profoundly shaped the private and public lives of our founding fathers and leaders, it also endured more scrutiny than any other document. It not only survived; it thrived! This book is part of the very fiber of who we are. But is it possible that we have even gone beyond the tipping point and are now sliding away from the foundations that made our country so strong?

A significant question we must ask ourselves is: Why is the Bible so deeply woven into the very fabric of America? The answer is simple and very clear: It is the people of our nation who have held this book as important and sacred. Because the Bible impacted their lives individually, it has become something of tremendous value in our society as a whole. As a result, it has impacted nearly every aspect of American life—past, present and future.

Today, the Bible is present in nearly every home and accessible to all in multiple formats online. The vast majority of Americans believe that it is the true, inspired Word of God. Mounting manuscript evidence and archeological discoveries continue to affirm its authority and accuracy. We can now prove that Scripture engagement is a vital key for spiritual growth. Modern translations have made it understandable and the vast majority of us believe it's time to get back to reading our Bibles.

So where will we go from here? What will be the future of the Bible in America? Will it regain the impact and influence it had in the past? Will our personal knowledge and understanding of it diminish or grow? Will it continue to shape our nation by impacting one life at a time?

These are important questions. How will we, as Americans answer? How will you, as an individual, respond to the opportunity to engage the Bible on a personal level?

APPENDIX

Religion and Civil Society:
A Review of 766 Studies Demonstrating
the Protective and Prosocial Effect of Religion
on Physical and Mental Health.

Byron R. Johnson
Institute for Studies of Religion
www.baylorisr.org

Extensive attention has been given in the United States to the subject of "civil society." Civil society has been referred to as that place in society where people make their home, sustain their marriages, raise their families, associate with friends, meet their neighbors, educate their children and worship their God. Many have wondered what role religious activities, involvements, practices, and beliefs may play in contributing to civil society. Thus, researchers are intrigued with empirical answers to how religious practices affects the way people live their lives. Indeed, over the last several decades scholars have conducted hundreds of studies that allow us to objectively answer many of these questions.

Unfortunately, this impressive body of empirical evidence often goes unnoticed—even by those that occupy the pews of America's houses of worship.

Let's take a look at the role of religion as a factor that protects Americans from harmful outcomes.[1]

Hypertension

Hypertension, which afflicts 50 million Americans, is defined as a sustained or chronic elevation in blood pressure. It is the most common of cardiovascular disorders and affects about 20 percent of the adult population. In recent years, epidemiological studies have found individuals who report higher levels of religious activities tend to have lower blood pressure. Seventy-six percent of the studies I reviewed found that religious activities or involvement tend to be linked with reduced levels of hypertension.

Mortality

A substantial body of research reveals an association between intensity of participation in religious activities and greater longevity. Studies reviewed examined the association between degree of religious involvement and life expectancy. Involvement in a religious community is consistently related to lower mortality and longer life spans.[2] I found that 75 percent of these published studies conclude that higher levels of religious involvement have a sizable and consistent relationship with greater longevity. This association is found independent of the effect of variables such as age, sex, race, education, and health.

Depression

Depression is the most common of all mental disorders and approximately 330 million people around the world suffer from it. People with depression are also at increased risk for use of hospital and medical services and for early death from physical causes.[3]

I reviewed over 100 studies examining the religion-depression relationship and we found that religious involvement tends to be associated with less depression in 68 percent of these articles. People who are frequently involved in religious activities and who highly value their religious faith are at reduced risk for depression.

Suicide

Suicide now ranks as the ninth-leading cause of death in the United States. A substantial literature documents that religious involvement (e.g. measured by frequency of religious attendance and frequency of prayer) is associated with less suicide, suicidal behavior, and suicidal ideation. In total, 87 percent of the studies reviewed on suicide found these beneficial outcomes.

Promiscuous Sexual Behaviors

Out-of-wedlock pregnancy, often a result of sexual activity among adolescents, is largely responsible for the nearly 25 percent of children age six or younger who are below the federal poverty line. Studies reviewed generally show those who are religious are less likely to engage in premarital sex or extramarital affairs or to have multiple sexual partners. In fact, approximately 97 percent of those studies reviewed reported significant correlations between increased religious involvement and lower likelihood of promiscuous sexual behaviors.

Drug and Alcohol Abuse

The abuse of alcohol and illicit drugs rank among the leading health and social concerns in the United States today. According to the National Institute for Drug Abuse, approximately 111 million persons are current alcohol users in the United States. About 32 million of these engage in binge drinking, 11 million Americans are heavy drinkers, and another 14 million are current users of illicit drugs.[4] I reviewed over 150 studies that examined the relationship between religiosity and drug use ($n=54$) or alcohol use (*n*=97) and abuse. The vast majority of these studies demonstrate that participation in religious activities is associated with less of a tendency to use or abuse drugs (87%) or alcohol (94%). The greater a person's religious involvement, the less likely s/he will initiate alcohol or drug use or have problems with these substances if used.

Delinquency

There is growing evidence that religious commitment and involvement helps protect youth from delinquent behavior and deviant activities[5] and lowers the risks of a broad range of delinquent behaviors, including both minor and serious forms of criminal behavior.[6] Additionally, there is growing evidence that religion can be used as a tool to help prevent high-risk urban youths from engaging in delinquent behavior.[7] Seventy-eight percent of these studies report reductions in delinquency and criminal acts are associated with higher levels of religious activity and involvements.

In sum, a review of the research on religious practices and health outcomes indicates that, in general, higher levels of religious involvement are associated with: reduced hypertension, longer survival, less depression, lower level of drug and alcohol use and abuse, less promiscuous sexual behaviors, reduced likelihood of suicide, lower rates of delinquency among youth, and reduced criminal activity among adults. This substantial body of empirical evidence demonstrates a very clear picture—those who are most involved in religious activities tend to do much better with respect to important and yet diverse outcome factors. Thus, aided by appropriate documentation, religiosity is now beginning to be acknowledged as a key protective factor, reducing the likelihood of a number of harmful outcomes.

Let's take a look at the role of religion as a factor that promotes prosocial behavior.

Well-Being

Well-being has been referred to as the positive side of mental health. Symptoms for well-being include happiness, joy, satisfaction, fulfillment, pleasure, contentment, and other indicators of a life that is full and complete.[8] I found that the vast majority of these studies, some 81 percent of the 99 studies reviewed, reported a positive association between religious involvement and greater happiness, life satisfaction, morale, positive affect or some other measure of well-being.

Hope/Purpose/Meaning in Life

Researchers have examined the role religion may or may not play in instilling hope and meaning, or a sense of purpose in life for adherents. Scholars have found, on the whole, a positive relationship between measures of religiosity and hope,[9] in varied clinical and nonclinical settings.[10] All total, 25 of the 30 studies reviewed (83%) document that increases in religious involvement or commitment are associated with having hope or a sense of purpose or meaning in life. Similarly, studies show that increasing religiousness is also associated with optimism as well as larger support networks, more social contacts, and greater satisfaction with support.[11]

Self-Esteem

Religion provides a basis for self-esteem that is not dependent upon individual accomplishments, relationships with others (e.g. "who you know"), or talent. In other words, a person's self-esteem is rooted in the individual's religious faith as well as the faith community as a whole. Of the studies we reviewed, 65 percent conclude that religious commitment and activities are related to increases in self-esteem.

Educational Attainment

The literature on the role of religious practices or religiosity on educational attainment represents a relatively recent development in the research literature. In the last decade or so a number of researchers have sought to determine if religion hampers or indeed enhances educational attainment. Even though the development of a body of evidence is just beginning to emerge, some 84 percent of the studies reviewed find religiosity or religious activities are positively correlated with improved educational attainment.[12]

To summarize, a review of the research on religious practices and various measures of well-being reveals that, in general, higher levels of religious involvement are associated with increased levels of: well-being, hope, purpose, meaning in life, and educational attainment. This review of 766 studies demonstrates the protective and prosocial effect of religion on physical and mental health outcomes is remarkably positive.

Conclusion

In most of the 766 studies reviewed, religiosity is measured in several different ways: frequency of church attendance, participation in religious activities, or self-reported indicators of the importance of faith in one's life. Rarely, however, have scholars asked about the frequency of Bible study, or the level of Scripture engagement. Studies examining the impact of levels religiosity or religious commitment on wide-ranging outcomes could no doubt benefit from the inclusion of variables that tap how often and the degree to which people read or study the Bible as well as other sacred texts. Is increasing biblical knowledge or literacy correlated in beneficial ways with some of the same outcomes as those documented in this current review? Might higher levels of biblical engagement predict one's religiosity, or even one's generosity? We do not yet have answers to these and many other important questions related to the Bible–but we certainly should.